SYLVAN CITIES

Also by Helen Babbs

Adrift: A Secret Life of London's Waterways

*My Garden, My City, and Me: Rooftop Adventures
in the Wilds of London*

SYLVAN CITIES
An urban tree guide

HELEN BABBS

Atlantic Books
London

First published in hardback in Great Britain in 2019 by Atlantic Books,
an imprint of Atlantic Books Ltd.

1 2 3 4 5 6 7 8 9

A CIP catalogue record for this book is available from the British Library.

Hardback ISBN: 978-1-78649-364-4
E-book ISBN: 978-1-78649-365-1

Printed in Great Britain by TJ International Ltd, Padstow, Cornwall

Atlantic Books
An Imprint of Atlantic Books Ltd
Ormond House
26–27 Boswell Street
London
WC1N 3JZ

www.atlantic-books.co.uk

sylva / *n.* (also **silva**) (pl. **sylvae** /-vi:/ or **sylvas**)

1 the trees of a region, epoch, or environment.

2 a treatise on or a list of such trees. [Latin *silva* 'a wood']

sylvan / *adj.* (also **silvan**) esp. *poet.*

1 a of the woods. **b** having woods; wooded.

Oxford English Dictionary

Contents

Beginning

When I first moved to London, aged eighteen, nature wasn't the thing that drew me in. But eighteen years later it has, strangely, become one of the things that has made me stay. I live on a boat, and the daily dramas played out by our local gulls, coots and geese are absorbing. I'm delighted that a grey wagtail visits me at home every late afternoon and, keen to know what's going on beyond the boat, I insist my partner tells me about the fox that's a regular at the pub where he drinks after work. I can even get excited about lichen. Each species has distinct preferences, which means their presence tells a story about the environment in which they grow. The acidic bark of a cherry tree, for instance, might have no lichen growing on it at all, except for a crust of green-grey *Phaeophyscia orbicularis* in the nitrogen-rich area around the base, where local dogs like to mark their territory. While nitrogen-loving lichens are a common sight, there are rarities here too, and I've found the joy of seeing something like a kingfisher is only made greater by the fact that it's hunting along an urban canal in the middle of the English capital. The juxtaposition of the natural and the artificial is what intensifies the pleasure, as is the sense that if these things can survive here, then so can I. The rare kingfisher, like the common lichen, shows that there's more to the inner city than just the human-made; that humans and wildlife can coexist and commingle.

Trees especially are reminders that the world is not ours alone. They're some of the most obvious examples of what's wild in the city, and some of the world's oldest and largest living organisms. I've come to appreciate the fact that London has so many of them: 8.4 million, to be precise. Massive but static, they line the streets I walk, overspill from the gardens I pass, sprout up along my rail routes and cycle paths, and furnish the parks and squares where I sometimes eat my lunch. They're what I stare at through the office window. In a hermetically sealed workplace, watching the way leaves brighten, darken and dance about helps bring the outside in.

For a long time I welcomed the presence of these quiet colossi into my life without knowing most of them by name. Did that matter? It's certainly possible to appreciate a tree's beauty, shade and shelter without knowing whether it's an alder, an elder, a lime or a beech. But, as with human relationships, an unnamed tree essentially remains a stranger. A name is the first step towards intimacy, so were I to make the effort to know their names, perhaps it would bring me closer to the trees.

⁙

This book germinated in 2016 and matured in 2018. In 2017 it grew and grew, rootling its way into almost everything I did. The result is a tree guide filtered through cities, as well as a city book filtered through trees, and it assumes that, when you're a beginner like me, and there are more than 60,000 species of tree in the world – including 500 different types of oak, 100 of pine and sixty of birch – simply knowing the family that a tree belongs to can sometimes be enough.

The sylvan city isn't one place, but several. While I did a lot of writing and research from home in London, I also travelled across the UK in search of stories about trees. I met Bournemouth's pines, Leeds' hazel woods and Milton Keynes' midsummer planes. I came across trees named after cities, such as the Bristol whitebeam and the Manchester poplar, as well as individuals that have become famous in their own right, like Glasgow's Argyle Street ash. I learned that alder and birch are true urban heroes, and I discovered how trees are as important for food and medicine as they are for furniture and firewood. I spent time with people who commute out of town and into the woods to work, and sought out inspiring tree-planters from the past. As well as being an illustrated guide that will help you identify some of the species you see around town every day, this is also the story of our cities' woody places and a search for where their wild things are.

⁙

It would be fair to think that the idea of the urban forest is a romantic one, a turn of phrase rather than a statement of fact, and it's true that the term 'sylvan city' is my attempt to sprinkle town trees with some fairy dust. But there is more to it than that.

Let's start 200 years ago, or thereabouts. That's not to say there weren't trees growing in towns before then, but 1800 was the beginning of the end of something. At that point our planet was, in general, a rural kind of place, with just two million people worldwide thought to be living in cities. Fast-forward a hundred years and that number had increased to thirty million. In Britain, three-quarters of people were town dwellers by the end of the 1800s, with one in five living in London. Conditions could be desperate and squalid, with uncertain employment and high rates of poverty, homelessness, disease and crime. In 'Winter Notes on Summer Impressions', an essay published after a trip to London in 1862, Fyodor Dostoevsky described a place as 'vast as an ocean', characterized, among other things, by 'terrifying districts such as Whitechapel with its half-naked, savage and hungry population', while social reformer Charles Booth's 1889 poverty map of the city marked out concentrations of people described as 'vicious, semi-criminal' and those who were suffering from 'chronic want'.

When you found yourself in a city, it was traditional to spend your days in mourning, plotting your escape. 'Thou hast pined and hungered after Nature, many a year, In the great City pent,' Samuel Taylor Coleridge wrote in a poem addressed to the essayist Charles Lamb in 1797, as if the metropolis were a prison and his city-dwelling friend an inmate. Eighty years later, the author of *Our British Trees and How to Know Them*, Francis George Heath, wrote that it wasn't until he moved to London that his 'latent love of nature was developed with full force, and became a passion'. Heath says, 'The absence of woods and fields gave rise to a painful longing to renew acquaintance with them on every possible occasion', suggesting that it was only through privation that he came to understand quite how much he loved the country. The urban was the hell that made the diminishing rural heavenly.

But as cities mushroomed and the Industrial Revolution roared, people living in them, and through it, became organized. In *A History of Nature Conservation in Britain*, David Evans describes protests about suffocating smogs and polluted watercourses, and dismay at the effluent filth of collieries and lead mines. Finally legislation was brought in to protect city dwellers. The 1863 Alkali Act started to control the heavy-chemicals industry, the Metropolitan Commons Act of 1866 protected all common land within twenty miles of large urban areas and guaranteed the general public the right to air and exercise, and a Public Health Act came into law in 1875. There was actually concern about urban pollution well before this. In 1664, John Evelyn, author of *Sylva, A Discourse of Forest-Trees and the Propagation of Timber in His Majesty's Dominions*, was already railing against a 'Hellish and dismal Cloud of SEACOAL' that was poisoning London. He included among his antidotes the planting of trees. Years later the Victorians seemed to agree with this prescription and became passionate city tree-planters. Some of our most handsome giants are with us today thanks to their efforts, including grand old horse chestnuts and soaring trees of heaven, as well as limes, poplars and planes. Many of our best-loved urban parks, such as Sefton Park in south Liverpool and Victoria Park in east London, opened around this time too.

Interest in, and concern for, urban nature wasn't widespread, but it gradually started to grow. Author W. H. Hudson was seriously observing the wildlife that a city could support at the end of the nineteenth century, publishing *Birds in London* in 1898, while the first book written specifically about the UK's city trees was published in 1910. Written by Angus Webster, it was called *Town Planting, And the trees, shrubs and other plants that are best adapted for resisting smoke*. But it was in the 1970s that urban conservation really took off in the UK, with organizations like Landlife in Liverpool taking concerted action on the ground. The urban nature-enthusiast's bible – *The Unofficial Countryside* by Richard Mabey – was published in 1973, the same year as the Tree Council's 'Plant a Tree in '73' campaign, which, among other things, was responsible for the crab-apple tree that grew in my grandparents' east-London garden. There are now numerous urban wildlife organizations and initiatives working across the UK, including ones dedicated to trees.

⁙

In contemporary cities – where flooding becomes more common, air and water quality can be abysmal, and the heat-island effect grows ever stronger, meaning that urban areas are significantly warmer than those surrounding them – trees do an awful lot of good. They limit the impact of heavy weather, be it intense sun or torrential rain, reduce air and water pollution and improve the soil. Urban ecology has become an important discipline, and those that practise it are busy assessing the size, role and economic worth of city trees, in a bid to persuade developers and policy-makers both to preserve the ones we already have and to consider planting many more.

There is also increasing evidence that regular access to nature – or a daily dose of 'vitamin G[reen]' – tangibly improves our physical and mental health, whether we purposely seek it out or swallow it up by accident. Natural England has published research which shows that taking part in nature-based activities can reduce anxiety, stress and depression, while the Royal Society for the Protection of Birds and the Wildlife Trusts have called on politicians to introduce a Nature and Wellbeing Act that puts nature at the heart of how decisions are made about issues such as health, housing and education. Frances Kuo, a professor from the University of Illinois, has collated research that proves just how essential parks and other green spaces are for city communities. Kuo's work shows that people from two of America's poorest urban neighbourhoods were found to suffer less violence and crime if they were living somewhere that had trees and grass, in comparison with those living in areas that were barren. Today it's widely agreed that the presence of trees makes towns and cities more habitable. As Charles Montgomery argues in his book *Happy City*, 'biological density must be the prerequisite for architectural density', if we're to create sustainable cities where people want to live.

::::

The term 'urban forest' was imported to Europe from the USA in the 1960s and started to take root in the UK in the 1980s.

At first it referred specifically to woodland in and around urban areas, but it has since grown to encompass single trees, groups of trees and woody areas. While a forest in the traditional sense is a geographical entity, the urban forest is a patchwork of different, unconnected landscapes and individuals. Urban forestry is a concept as much as a physical thing, and it's cultural as much as it is natural. It recognizes that trees have spiritual worth as well as practical value. And this is the key: urban forestry is about people as much as it's about plants, and one of its main aims is the welfare of urban residents. Where trees in a conifer plantation have commercial worth, the trees in a city have amenity value. The point of them is to please you and me, to bring us joy and improve our quality of life. The urban forest is real and it is romantic. The two ways of seeing city trees are not at odds.

Trees and cities

LEAF GUIDE

Common alder p.18   Common ash p.26   Common beech p.36

Silver birch p.46   Butterfly bush p.56   Wild cherry p.64

Common elder p.76   English elm p.88   Common fig p.98

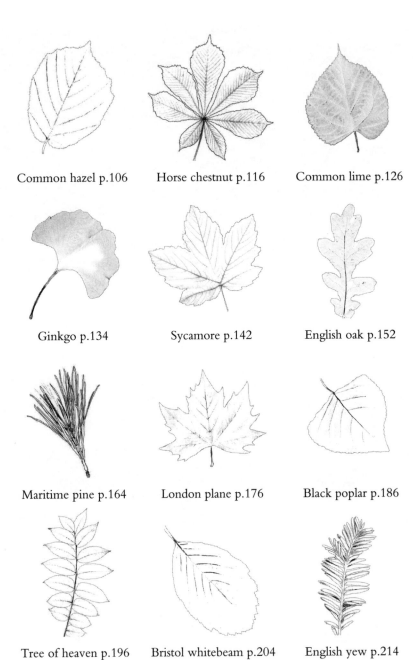

Common hazel p.106   Horse chestnut p.116   Common lime p.126

Ginkgo p.134   Sycamore p.142   English oak p.152

Maritime pine p.164   London plane p.176   Black poplar p.186

Tree of heaven p.196   Bristol whitebeam p.204   English yew p.214

The alders

There are several different types of alder tree – around thirty – and all of them enhance soil fertility. They also all have catkins and small, woody, cone-like fruits, which together make alders easy to pick out from other trees, especially in winter when they have lost all their leaves.

COMMON ALDER
Alnus glutinosa

'*Alnus*' means red, which refers to the fact that alder wood 'bleeds' when cut, turning red on exposure to the air; '*glutinosa*', meanwhile, reveals that this tree has buds and young leaves that are sticky.

Shape is slender and conical, becoming more straggled with age. (Fig. 1)

Leaves are dark green, round and leathery; never pointed, but sometimes indented at the tip. (Fig. 2)

Bark is grey-brown and finely fissured.

Flowers are drooping purplish catkins (male), erect green catkins (female), both on the same tree.

Fruit are small, woody cones stuffed with tiny seeds. (Fig. 3)

Found by water and marshy ground, as well as in landfill sites and reclamation projects.

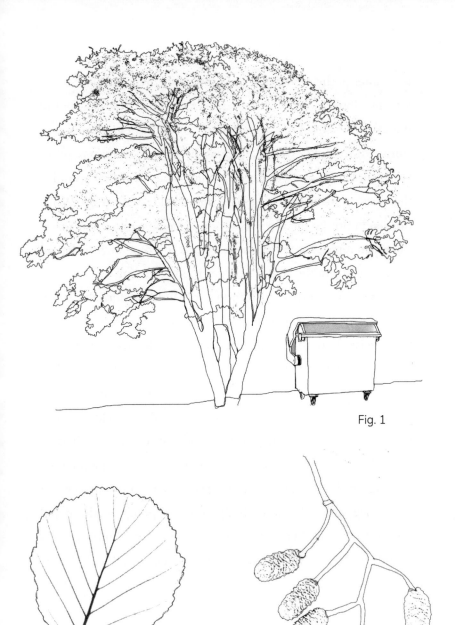

Fig. 1

Fig. 2

Fig. 3

It's winter in the sylvan city and most of the trees are bare. From afar they look gaunt, absent even – tree-shaped holes cut out of the greyscale sky. Up close, they're as solid as ever, their dark trunks rimed with wet. Early, on the coldest mornings when your hands ache and your breath billows out of you like smoke, the trees' high-up branches flash and crackle with frost. While this might not be the obvious season to begin a journey through the urban forest, some trees have traits at this time of year that set them apart from the rest. The alder is one of them.

It was a February afternoon of insistent drizzle when I first learned how to pick alder out from a crowd. The day was melancholy but mild, requiring wellington boots and waterproofs rather than gloves and a hat. I was walking in Wick Wood beside the canalized River Lea, on the outer edges of Hackney in east London. Once known as Wick Field, this was planted into a small community woodland in the late 1990s. I didn't have a route mapped out around the wood. I'd exited my floating canal-boat home with no plan other than to stretch out my sea legs and unbend my body. It was dripping overhead and soft underfoot, and the air inside the wood seemed moister than outside it. There's always white noise in a city – traffic, industry, people – but in Wick Wood it was quiet. Even without their leaves, the close-packed trees and shrubs formed a soundproof barrier between me and the world beyond.

Everything seemed dormant or dead, so it was a surprise when I came upon a tree that was free of leaves, but busy with birds. The birdwatcher camping out in an adjacent bush made sense, as there was plenty to see. He explained that the birds were siskins and the tree was an alder, a species beloved for the cone-like, seed-packed fruits it wears all through winter. Looking at the tree, I could see that it was indeed studded with tiny, woody cones and I knew this was unusual – as a rule, cones are found on conifers or cone-bearing firs, trees that tend to keep their leaves all year round. The naked alder was clearly not an evergreen, and so these cones were a feature that made it stand out.

The common alder is deciduous or broadleaved, which means it sheds its leaves in autumn and grows new ones in spring. Revisiting Wick Wood a few months later, I learned that alder leaves are distinctive: dark green, rounded, almost the shape of a tennis racket, sometimes with a gentle indent at the tip. But it's definitely when the alder loses them that it is easiest to spot. Shaking off its leathery summer coat, the tree reveals that its branches have become covered in flowers. It's not blossom, in the apple or cherry-tree sense, but rather that the tree is decked with drooping, purplish catkins and upright, green ones, which eventually ripen into those telltale dark-brown cones. Legend has it that Robin Hood's camouflaging outfit was dyed using a green pigment made from these blooms. The drooping catkins are male, the upright ones female. Like many of the species we'll meet in the urban forest, flowers of both sexes grow on the same tree, making the alder 'monoecious', or a hermaphrodite.

⁙

It's neat that the alder sits at the beginning of this alphabetically organized book, because where it grows marks the start of a new story. It may be relatively short-lived – it averages about sixty years, where some trees, like the yew, can live for centuries – but it does a lot for us in its lifetime, and even after its death. Like all plants, alder photosynthesizes – this invisible process not only provides fuel for the plant, but is also responsible for the oxygen, food, fibres, medicines and timber that we need to live.

What makes the alder different is that it's a pioneer, one of a small number of tree species that prepares the way for future forests. It uses the carbohydrates produced during photosynthesis in a very particular way – it provides its self-made sugars to bacteria that live on its roots. In turn, the bacteria absorb nitrogen from the atmosphere and provide it to the tree. In this way, the alder and its ally feed each other, at the same time cleansing the air of pollutants and enriching the earth with nutrients, clearing the way for other varieties of tree to take root. The alder's ability to improve air and soil quality in this way makes it an urban hero, and landscape architects call on it when they have contaminated land to reclaim. 'Phytoremediation' is a way of using plants to restore balance, and an abandoned site might be planted with alders as part of its transformation from industrial to recreational.

Alder has a close connection with water too, and the fact that I found my first one growing in the urban but also riparian Wick Wood makes a lot of sense. It's able to grow close to watercourses and in waterlogged ground because, as well as hosting those special nitrogen-fixing bacteria, alder roots have a system of air ducts that allow oxygen to flow, even underwater. These roots can also act like underground scaffolding and prevent soil erosion, and water-tolerant alder is planted along with willow to help keep riverbanks intact. No wonder the poet Kathleen Jamie turns to the alder in an 'age of rain', seeking advice on 'a way to live on this damp ambiguous earth' in her poem named after the tree.

It's not only in life that the alder is heroic – once it is felled for timber, alder wood is soft and porous, and is only durable when kept wet. Rather than rotting, this timber is most effective when it's waterlogged, which is why much of Venice is built on alder piles cut from strong tree trunks. As Italo Calvino suggests in *Invisible Cities*, 'Nothing of the city touches the earth except those long flamingo legs on which it rests.' Alder is part of Venice's strength and support. It helps to hold the city in place.

ANOTHER ALDER WORTH KNOWING

In the *Collins Tree Guide* – an essential reference book for any tree-lover – dendrologist Owen Johnson describes the Italian alder (*Alnus cordata*) as 'a plant with vigour and polish'. It's fast-growing, capable of reaching twenty-five metres, where the common alder can usually achieve just twenty metres. It has conspicuous catkins in winter that can be up to ten centimetres long, and its large cones are red before they turn brown. The Italian alder also has glossy, heart-shaped leaves, smooth grey bark and a tidier, more slender shape. It comes into leaf early and loses that foliage late. It's heat-, drought- and pollution-tolerant, making it a popular choice for urban streets, car parks and shelter belts.

The ashes

The ashes are a large, widespread group of trees – or 'genus' – possibly more than sixty members strong. Ash trees are usually male or female, but sometimes they swap sex or are both. All of them have compound leaves made up of leaflets arranged along a central stalk, and produce seeds enclosed inside a papery wing. These hang in bunches on the trees throughout winter, long after the leaves have been shed.

COMMON ASH

Fraxinus excelsior

Both 'ash' and '*fraxinus*' stem from words meaning spear. This makes sense, as ash wood is strong and elastic, and was once an important material for making weaponry.

Shape is large but slender, with a rounded crown, a long, straight trunk and open, arching branches. (Fig. 4)

Leaves are compound, with elliptical, toothed leaflets arranged in opposite pairs along the leaf stem. (Fig. 5)

Bark is pale grey, darkening and splitting with age.

Flowers are sexually ambiguous; small purple and green tufts burst open at the tip of the twig.

Fruit are seeds enclosed inside a narrow wing, which ripens from green to light brown. (Fig. 6)

Found in parks and city streets, including in Glasgow.

Fig. 5

Fig. 6

The first tree to lose its leaves in autumn and the last to re-clothe come spring, flowering before it does so, the common ash is easiest to identify in winter. Without foliage, the tree's long, elegant trunk and loose, up-and-down arching branches with their silver-grey skin are most visible. But it is the tree's fruit and next year's buds that will help you single it out. Known as a 'key', each fruit looks like a papery, flattened pea pod. The seed is enclosed inside this casing, which is essentially a wing, aerodynamically designed to catch the wind and glide off to new ground. The ash keys ripen on the tree, turning from pale green to buff-brown, and hang in dense bunches throughout the colder months. As late winter melts into spring and other trees gradually come back into leaf, the ash remains resolute: bare, except for its bunches of keys and its increasingly succulent, matt-black buds.

⁙

Wistfully known as 'Venus of the woods' – that mystical, forested place where the oak is considered king and the beech, queen – ash is actually a tree of the city as much as the countryside. It's currently facing two serious threats: one a microscopic fungus that causes a condition called 'ash dieback', first recorded in the UK in 2012; the other a destructive emerald ash-borer beetle from north-eastern Asia, which is yet to reach the UK, but has been causing havoc in the United States. Both could have a significant impact on the future shape of our urban forests: it's thought that very few of the UK's 128 million ash trees will be spared by the ash-dieback fungus. But, for now, the ash is a common sight, especially in Scotland's biggest and busiest city.

Glasgow – or '*glaschu*' in Gaelic, meaning 'dear green place' – is one of the most densely wooded urban centres in Britain, with 112 trees per hectare, almost twice the average sixty to be found in English cities and towns, and significantly more than in Edinburgh. If you were to stitch all of Glasgow's trees' foliage together into one giant leaf, its total area would be 112 square kilometres – roughly the size of Jersey. There are estimated to be 250,000 ash trees in the city, and when you walk through its parks and streets, the ash is the tree you'll encounter most often.

We know these precise statistics about Glasgow and its ash trees because the city's forest has been surveyed using open-source i-Tree software. Such surveys don't just document the species found in a town or simply measure their extent, but also attempt to quantify and put an economic value on the practical benefits that trees provide for a city. This work is largely being done in the context of climate change, and it's motivated by the fact that urban trees are one way to strengthen local resilience in the face of high winds, heavy rain, heatwave and drought. As well as being Glasgow's most common tree, the ash has been found to trap the most rainfall, catching it on its leaves and absorbing it into its tissues for use in respiration. Glasgow's ash trees intercept 109,000 cubic metres of rainwater each year, relieving pressure on sewers and so saving the city £147,000 in sewerage charges annually. Combined, Glasgow's two million trees are thought to be worth around £4 billion, and to provide £4.4 million worth of 'ecosystem services' each year, which includes carbon capture and storage, pollution removal and shading, as well as flood relief.

Urban trees cost money to manage and maintain, but it's relatively new to talk about what living trees give back, in terms of cold, hard cash. It's an example of a trend towards viewing flora and fauna as 'natural capital'. The Office for National Statistics has estimated that nature is worth more than £1.5 trillion to the UK economy. It's an extraordinary, attention-grabbing figure that ecologists hope will help secure our environment's future by using the financial language that businesses and politicians understand.

We have, of course, been talking for centuries about trees in terms of what they can do for us. We know a surprising amount about tree cover in 1086, for example, because the Domesday Book recorded coppice woods for timber production and wood pasture for livestock, in order to establish whether the land had value and was therefore liable to be taxed. And ash has long been celebrated as a useful source of firewood and charcoal, as well as for being tough and shock-absorbent, an elastic blond wood from which hockey sticks and hammers are made. But contemporary phrases such as 'ecosystem services' and 'natural capital' are different, and have a tendency to rob what's wild of its poetry, using corporate-speak that discounts everything that can't be assessed in pounds and pence. The way we define something shapes how we go on to treat it. With a capital-focused way of thinking, there's a danger that an ash tree that is deemed uneconomical – because it's not absorbing enough carbon dioxide, say, or intercepting enough rainwater – will have little hope for it but the chop, discounting the fact that some of the most precious things it provides are priceless.

Trees can be totems as much as they are plants. We use them to symbolize endurance and self-sufficiency, wisdom and enlightenment, generations past and those to come. Trees can also be where we locate our gods, our muses and our demons. In Scandinavia, the ash tree is associated with magic – Yggdrasil, the Norse world tree, was an ash. Yggdrasil's canopy stretched up into heaven and its roots reached down into the underworld, forming a connection between our world and that of the gods. The first man on Earth was called Askr, which means ash tree in Old Norse. Askr and his female counterpart, Embla, were created by the gods from two tree trunks they found washed up on the seashore.

While knowing the number of ash trees in Glasgow is exciting, as are statistics that show the positive impact they have collectively, it is fables like these about Yggdrasil, Askr and Embla that resonate with me. It suggests the boundary between me and the tree is not as clearly defined as it might at first seem, and that it's possible to look at plants in a way that's spiritual more than practical. In *The Living Mountain*, Scottish author Nan Shepherd gives us permission to experience the natural world intensely and intimately, but not necessarily by always understanding how it works. Describing the water that spurts out of the top of a mountain, she admits that the more she gazes at the 'sure and unremitting surge', the more baffled she becomes. 'I don't understand it. I cannot fathom its power.' Shepherd later writes that simply to look on anything 'with the love that penetrates to its essence, is to widen the domain of being in the vastness of non-being. Man has no other reason for his existence.' She was a naturalist who relished the mysterious, who understood the importance of, sometimes, simply standing in awe.

::::

One of Glasgow's best-loved ash trees can be found outside Franklin Terrace on Argyle Street in Finnieston. It grows close up against a traditional four-storey stone tenement block, reaching well above roof height. On a street that otherwise has few plants, this house-hugging ash has become a local landmark, protected by a tree preservation order. In his 1935 book, *From Glasgow's Treasure Chest*, James Cowan wrote about how graceful the Argyle Street ash tree was, describing it 'as straight as a ship's mast'. Cowan explains that the ash was planted by accident some time in the 1850s, when residents of the then newly built tenement brought home some primrose roots from a holiday and planted them in their narrow front garden. An ash seed must have been nestled in the transplanted soil. In time, it grew and was allowed to stay. Already well over 150 years old, the tree could live to see 400, although this would be a great age for an ash: on average they live for about 200 years.

To look out of a window and straight into a tree is a particular experience, and one that will change with the time of day and year, and with the weather. In spring and summer the sun must filter in weakly through the Argyle Street ash's feathery foliage, giving shady tenement rooms an underwater feel, and turning complexions a bilious sort of sea-green. At night, the tree might be electrically lit and rocked by the wind. And there will be moments when its arching limbs begin tapping insistently. In an essay about artist Alex Katz's oil painting, *Night Branch*, Dylan Trigg describes the irregular but constant rhythm of a tree brushing against an apartment window, and the shifting flecks of lamplight that the branches haphazardly let in. The boundary between inside and out, between the domestic and the not, becomes blurry. The window is a threshold, and the tree taps, taps, taps, 'as though summoning you to another place'.

ANOTHER ASH WORTH KNOWING

The Raywood ash (*Fraxinus angustifolia*) is an exuberantly frothy, narrow-leaved tree that looks like an ash crossed with a willow. It was fashionable in the 1970s and 1980s, and was planted widely as a street tree during both decades. The way the foliage sits on the tree has something of the loose bubble-perm about it. If you look closely, you'll see the leaves cluster together in shaggy groups the size and shape of cheerleaders' pom-poms. It's also known as the claret ash, because that bubbly green foliage can deepen through gold to dark wine-red in autumn.

The beeches

There are northern beeches and southern beeches, evergreen beeches and various beech cultivars. Most have nuts clothed in coarse, hairy jackets, which are edible but bitter. The northerners all have smooth, elephantine skin. Beech makes excellent firewood and charcoal, while cellulose fibres derived from beech trees are used to make the silky, semi-synthetic fabric known as modal, which is marketed as an alternative to cotton.

COMMON BEECH

Fagus sylvatica

It's thought the early books of northern Europe might have been written on thin slithers of beech bark. In modern German, beech is '*Buche*' and book is '*Buch*', while in Swedish '*bok*' means both beech and book.

Shape is tall, spreading and muscular, but shallow-rooted and prone to topple. (Fig. 7)

Leaves are green and oval, with a pointed end and a wavy edge. (Fig. 8)

Bark is skin-smooth, pinkish-grey and elephant-like.

Flowers are small round catkins (male), erect clusters (female), both on the same tree.

Fruit are glossy brown nuts, encased in a tough, hairy jacket. (Fig. 9)

Found in urban woodlands and parks.

Fig. 7

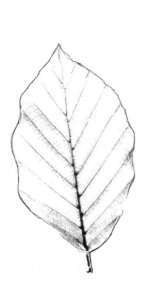

Fig. 8

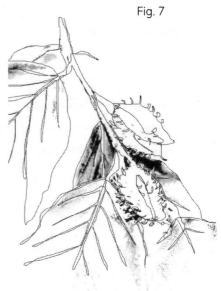

Fig. 9

The beech is one of the sylvan city's most physically impressive trees, one you might see growing in parkland or on wooded urban edges, places where it has room to stretch out. This tree has heft, it soars. It has a broad, domed crown and, when in leaf, a mature beech's wide-spreading canopy casts a dense shade that starves other plants of light. It has a muscular trunk and skin-smooth, pinkish-grey bark. When I look at an aged beech I almost always think of elephants.

Below ground, the tree's snaking, shallow roots can sometimes be glimpsed bulging just beneath the soil's surface. Looking down, as well as up, is important when it comes to identifying trees – the earth around a beech doesn't just boil with roots, it's also likely to be strewn with cast-off nuts and carpeted with browning leaves. Before the leaves drop in autumn they rust and crisp, their green flesh made metal. Come spring, unfurled new leaves will be lime-green, citrusy and soft.

⁑

Since common beech is a tree of the woods more than it is one of the streets, it's a species to seek out when you're craving a change of scene. As much as I enjoy living in London, it's always tempting to shake it off and head for the peripheries, at least for a while. There are woodlands preserved for this purpose, authentically ancient but within easy reach of town, so close you can slope there and back in a day. Burnham Beeches covers 220 hectares of Buckinghamshire greenbelt, twenty miles west of the English capital. It can be called an urban forest – or a forest for urbanites

– not only because it's reasonably close to the metropolis, but because it's owned and managed by the Corporation of the City of London. Once working wood pasture, it was bought by the Corporation in 1880 and has been managed by it ever since.

Today Burnham Beeches is a place for picnics and woodland walks. Protected as a Site of Special Scientific Interest and a National Nature Reserve, its beautiful beech pollards are thought to average 400 years old or more. The proximity of film studios like Shepperton and Pinewood mean that it's sometimes also used as a set – parts of *Robin Hood, Prince of Thieves* were filmed in the forest, for instance, and it provided shelter for a fleeing Harry, Hermione and Ron in *Harry Potter and the Deathly Hallows*. But woodlands like this were once much more practical places, an important source of food, fuel, fibre and wood for surrounding villages, towns and cities. Pollarding is a management technique that sees a tree cut to between six and fifteen feet above the ground, leaving a permanent trunk – or 'bolling' – from which an indefinite crop of wood will sprout, high enough up to be safe from browsing deer. Beech wood bends and turns easily, and is a favourite of furniture-makers. It also burns hot, and makes a fine charcoal.

Less practically but more poetically, beech has long been favoured by lovers, who like to carve sweet nothings into its bark and then watch their hopes and dreams – or 'arborglyphs' – swell over the years with the expanding tree. Smooth trunks make good canvases, and a walk through etched-upon beeches can be noisy with voices from the past. In *The Ash and the Beech* the naturalist Richard Mabey describes this as 'not really tree abuse ... nor always a compulsion to leave one's mark on the world. More ... the world's leaving a mark on you.' Salisbury Plain is littered with arborglyphs carved by homesick soldiers stationed there during the First and Second World Wars, as is the Western Front in northern France. In parts of the United States it's possible to trace the journeys made by lonesome shepherds who emigrated there from the Basque Country in the nineteenth century by following the trail of tree carvings they left behind. Their arborglyphs feature words, dates and pictures, including titillating ones of naked women.

::::

Beech shares the first part of its botanical name with an enigmatic Celtic god of beech trees called Fagus, who was revered in the French Pyrenees. We have a long history of tree worship like this, seeing trees first as animate, god-like beings in their own right, then as the leafy abodes of sylvan deities and tree spirits. This makes sense when we consider how wooded the world we inhabited once was, what benevolent providers of goods and services trees are and how mysterious and long-lived.

While tree worship is no longer common, there is still something supernatural about woods. From a young age, we learn that the forest is a place of strange encounters, of terrors, joys and transformations. Think of Snow White, Red Riding Hood and Hansel and Gretel, of Enid Blyton's enchanted wood and her faraway tree, or of the wild wood in the *Wind in the Willows*. Magic forests aren't just for children, an obvious example being the tricksy wood outside Athens in *A Midsummer Night's Dream*, home to shapeshifting hobgoblins and warring fairies, and where humans can be translated into beasts. The idea of going into the woods to hide, escape or experiment with a new identity is a potent one. Forests are useful places for exploring our fears and desires.

This is true, too, of George Orwell's *Keep the Aspidistra Flying*, first published in 1936. The aspidistra was a popular and extremely hardy house-plant, one that was able to thrive in stuffy environments with little light or air, and is used by Orwell in sarcastic reference to the English middle classes. The novel's main character, Gordon Comstock, is a poet living on the poverty line in London. His girlfriend, Rosemary – ever the optimist, in the face of her gloomy lover – suggests that they take a restorative day-trip right out of town, 'somewhere you can walk all day and hardly meet a soul'. The couple travel by train and bus to Burnham Beeches and, before it all inevitably goes wrong, they are extravagantly happy among the old beech trees, content to head in any direction 'so long as it was away from London'. It's winter, sunny, crisp and still, and fallen beech leaves form 'folds of copper-coloured silk' into the distance. Rosemary wades knee-deep into the leaf litter, glorying in all that gold, while Gordon teases that it's 'just the colour of tomato soup'. Once they emerge from the woods, the couple are destined to be ripped off in a hotel restaurant and to fail to consummate their relationship, but while they are within the beech trees' shelter they have licence to do as they please.

Orwell presents forest and city as antipodal, with the woods idealized and adopted as a place of freedom. Standing among giants, Gordon and Rosemary find immense comfort in the seeming simplicity of an old beech wood. While they don't worship the trees they encounter, there is something reverential about their appreciation. I know how they feel. A 400-year-old beech tree is awe-inspiring, while the forest can offer those of us who wander into its charmed precincts a release, albeit temporary, from real life.

ANOTHER BEECH WORTH KNOWING

The copper beech (*Fagus sylvatica* 'Purpurea') was popular with the Victorians, who planted it widely in city streets, parks and squares. It has dark, purple-red leaves that have a peculiar bronze-green hue. They become richly copper-coloured in autumn, and often remain on the lower branches until new leaves appear the following spring.

AND A BEECH-LIKE TREE

The common hornbeam (*Carpinus betulus*) is similar-looking to the common beech, especially the foliage, although the hornbeam's leaves are smaller and more pleated. Also like beech, the hornbeam's bark is smooth and grey, but it's more sinuous, developing snaking vertical ridges with age. What sets the hornbeam apart are its attractive strings of nuts, which are clothed with a profusion of papery, leaf-like bracts and hang from the tree like green garlands. 'Horn' means hard and 'beam' means wood in Old English, and the hornbeam's strong, creamy-coloured timber is still used for furniture and flooring. It's a tree most often found growing in peri-urban woods and parks, but also along some city streets, especially its tidier cultivars.

The birches

The birches are small, fast-growing but short-lived trees, with papery, finely striped bark and an airy canopy. The male flowers are eye-catching: long catkins appear in autumn and adorn the bare branches throughout winter, swelling in spring when they release their abundant pollen. These trees have been widely cultivated as ornamentals because of their decorative catkins and exceptionally pale skin, which Robert Frost described as 'snow-white' in his poem 'Birches'.

SILVER BIRCH
Betula pendula

'*Betula*' is derived from a word meaning shine, likely in reference to birch trees' silky bark, while '*pendula*' means hanging down, a nod to this species' weeping profile.

Shape is slim and spumy; thin branches have distinctly drooping, or weeping, tips. (Fig. 10)

Leaves are small, toothed teardrops, with a tapered end and rounded base. (Fig. 11)

Bark is silvery with horizontal pinstripes, developing triangular fissures and dark cracks.

Flowers are long yellowish catkins (male), slender green-then-brown catkins (female), both on the same tree.

Fruit are tiny seeds with papery wings. (Fig. 12)

Found in streets, parks and gardens everywhere.

Fig. 10

Fig. 11

Fig. 12

Like alder, the silver birch is a pioneer, and one of the first trees to take root when open land starts to become wood. It's slender but sturdy, and always hungry for light. At home in inhospitable environments, the birch is as well suited to cities as it is to wildernesses. It's one of the urban forest's prettiest and most easily recognizable members, with its delicate burgundy branches and white bark. This skin splits with age, gradually becoming roughly printed with dark geometric shapes. A gnarled silver birch looks as if it's starting to bulge at the seams, as though ageing flesh is seething beneath silken skin and occasionally bursting through. The tree's small teardrop leaves have attractively serrated edges and hang from thin boughs that gently weep. The foliage is loose rather than closely packed, creating a shaggy, airy canopy that you can see the sky through.

If in doubt, the final feature that makes the silver birch easy to identify are its male flowers. Catkins decorate the tree throughout winter, and swell to become long and dangling come spring, when they release their pollen. Fertilized female flowers ripen into fruit, and a single birch's annual crop can be up to one million powder-fine seeds strong. These are dispersed by the wind, flying off to the next exposed patch of ground that's ripe to become wooded.

You'll see stands of birch trees all over town, along busy streets and rail routes, as well as in more secluded parts. It's one of the most common trees in central London, artfully planted outside cultural behemoths like Tate Modern and the Barbican. The first silver birch I got to know grew in a suburban front garden, while many of the ones I meet today are treated more like pot plants than trees, placed outside cafés and bars in huge troughs.

::::

The birch's black-and-white bark has a graphic quality that makes it a design favourite, but this tree gives city dwellers more than aesthetic pleasure: it offers us protection too. There are plenty of things that make urban areas unwelcoming to living things, but bad air is perhaps the principal one. In the UK, 40,000 lives are estimated to be cut short every year because of air pollution – babies, children and the elderly are most vulnerable to its effects. And here's why the silver birch is more than just a pretty face – while all trees are imagined to improve the air, studies show that birch is one of the best.

A collaboration between the University of Lancaster and the BBC show *Trust Me, I'm a Doctor* demonstrated how and why the birch is a saviour for those of us who live in areas plagued by traffic. Scientists placed a row of potted young silver birch trees along a pavement in Lancaster, with the busy A9 on one side and four terraced houses on the other. Next to those houses were four more, which were identical, except that they lacked a birch barrier between them and the road.

At the beginning of the experiment the television and computer screens in the front rooms of all eight houses were cleaned, and the devices were then left on standby for a fortnight. In this dormant state, they became excellent dust traps. Two weeks later, identical areas of each of the screens in all eight houses were wiped down, and the dust collected was analysed for iron-bearing particulates. The scientists were astounded by what they found. The particulate pollution inside the four houses with the tree screen was 50–60 per cent lower than in those without.

There are two reasons why the silver birch proved so effective at protecting the houses from particulate pollution. The tree's loose, relatively sparse canopy allows air to circulate and flow freely through it, while its leaves are covered in microscopic hairs and ridges that help to trap passing particles. When it rains, the pollution is washed off the leaves, freeing them to catch more. The scientists concluded that while the silver birch is in leaf, it acts as an excellent pollution filter. This isn't true of all trees. Taller species, with denser canopies of more tightly packed leaves, can act as pollution traps rather than pollution filters, if the built-up street they line is canyon-shaped. By obstructing wind flow, they can prevent emissions from escaping and, in the short term, actually make air quality worse, not better. However, trees are not to blame for the atrocious air pollution that plagues modern cities: the internal combustion engine is. The solution is to cut petrol- and diesel-burning traffic, not trees, and in the meantime to plant more birches.

::::

The silver birch does much for us while it lives and breathes. It also does much for us once it's dead. Like most, if not all, trees, it can be cut down and reborn as timber. Solid birch wood is a thing of beauty in its own right – pale and silky, just as it's a pale and silky tree – but, with layering and the addition of glue, birch has the potential to become so much more: an elastic material as much like plastic and metal as it is like wood.

The ancient Egyptians were producing a plywood of sorts back in 2600 BCE, but it was the invention of mechanized saws in the 1790s that guaranteed it would eventually become dreamily universal and cheap, the curvaceous stuff that chairs, prefabs, dinghies and skateboards are made of. Plywood is now increasingly popular with open-source digital designers, not least because of the rise of fully automated, computer numerical controlled machines – known as CNC machines – that can cut it into pre-programmed shapes. It was even considered important enough to get its own show at London's Victoria and Albert Museum in 2017. The exhibition was an attempt by the art and design institution to improve the status of an overlooked but revolutionary material.

It was the V&A exhibition that opened my eyes to the wonders of plywood, and taught me how it is made by glueing together very thin slices of wood, or 'veneers', with the grain of each slice running in an alternate direction. A birch tree is transformed into these veneers using a rotating lathe, which unwinds the trunk into a single thin sheet of wood. A trunk with a diameter of twenty-four centimetres will produce a twenty-metre-long sheet, and today a log of that size can be fully peeled in as little as seven seconds. The process recalls a pencil being sharpened, and the resulting sheet looks like stiff fabric, pale pinkish-grey and faintly patterned with the grain of the wood. The unwound birch on display in the V&A was presented like a huge, half-unfurled scroll.

Plywood has been used in engineering projects since the 1860s, manufactured on an industrial scale since the 1870s and was in wide use by the 1880s. For a long time it fought against a reputation of being inferior to solid wood, but that began to change in the 1920s, when designers became experimental and were no longer shy about exploiting the potential of plywood to be manipulated into modernist shapes. A bentwood armchair designed by Alvar Aalto in 1932 has a seven-ply birch seat and a four-ply birch frame, with solid birch-wood struts. Called the Paimio Chair, it was designed for use in the patients' lounge of a sanatorium in Finland, where residents could recline in a position where their lungs would be open and they could breathe deeply. The chairs were specifically to be positioned beside windows with views of the sanatorium's surrounding woodland. This was a chair made from birch that was designed for looking at trees.

The V&A exhibition was full of creations like Aalto's chair, some more fanciful than others. A collection of birch bathing suits from the 1930s – part of a PR stunt to advertise waterproof ply – was on display alongside various handsome tea chests, dating from 1950 to the 1970s. Plywood was favoured for chests like these because it didn't contaminate the taste of the tea. It was also resistant to warping, was lightweight and could be shipped flat-packed to tea-growing regions. Britain's tea industry meant that we were once the largest importer of plywood in the world. But the most magical object in the exhibition was a book bound with three-ply birch, leather and green silk cord. It was a copy of the *Aurora Australis*, the first book ever to be written, illustrated, printed, published and bound in the Antarctic. Ernest Shackleton and his crew took a printing press on their 1907–9 *Nimrod* expedition as a way of giving themselves something to do during the polar nights. They recycled their plywood provision cases into bindings for their self-made books.

Today, silver birch is not only a popular and practical planting choice for city streets, parks and gardens, but also continues to be part of everyday life in its versatile plywood form. But, rather than being work-a-day, birch was once seen as sacred by pagan and Germanic tribes, who believed it had powers of purification and renewal. This reputation still stands. As a living tree, silver birch purifies the air, removing particulate pollution so that we can breathe more easily. As timber transformed into veneers, it can be glued and moulded into all manner of forms, renewed and capable of a long and equally useful second life.

ANOTHER BIRCH WORTH KNOWING

The Himalayan birch (*Betula utilis*) hails from the Himalayas, where it's found growing at high altitude and in heavy snow. The white bark was used in ancient times as a kind of parchment for sacred Sanskrit texts – '*utilis*' refers to its usefulness. This species has since become a fashionable choice for towns and cities. It's small, slender and frothy, like the classic silver birch, with similarly shaped leaves, but its bark is different: more papery and peeling, still pale, but often flushed peach. Different varieties of Himalayan birch have differently coloured bark – *jacquemontii*'s is the brightest white, as though thickly painted with the finest emulsion paint.

The butterfly bushes

The butterfly bushes form a large genus of flowering plants. Most are low-growing shrubs, but some have been known to reach thirty metres high and to adopt decidedly tree-like forms. They have dazzling flower spikes that are nectar-rich and honey-scented. Popular and vigorous ornamentals, the butterfly bushes are planted in gardens to attract pollinating insects such as bees, as well as Lepidoptera.

BUTTERFLY BUSH
Buddleja davidii

'*Buddleja*' was posthumously named after the Reverend Adam Buddle, an English botanist who lived from 1662 to 1715, while '*davidii*' celebrates Father Armand David, a French plant-collector who first encountered the butterfly bush while journeying through China on scientific missions in the mid-1800s.

Shape is shrubby and many-stemmed, sometimes tall and woody. (Fig. 13)

Leaves are green-grey, long and narrow, arranged in opposite pairs along the stem. (Fig. 14)

Bark is pale brown, becoming fissured with age.

Flowers are bright purple with an orange eye, clustered tightly into large, jubilant spires. (Fig. 15)

Fruit are tiny seeds housed inside a small capsule.

Found in gardens and anywhere rubbly that it can take root.

Fig. 13

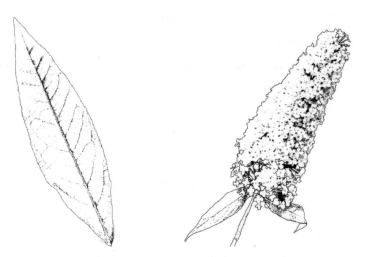

Fig. 14

Fig. 15

The butterfly bush shouldn't be in this book. There are several reasons why, including that it isn't a tree. But it seems appropriate that it would wheedle its way in here. The buddleia is one of those tenacious urban plants that seems able to grow just about anywhere, and delights and offends in equal measure. I love it and its brazen ways; and while many butterfly bushes are indeed shrub-shaped, there are also plenty that could be called tree-like, both in size and in silhouette.

What is it that makes ash or birch a tree, but buddleia a bush? It's to do with the main stem or trunk, and specifically there being more than one of them. If a plant is multi-stemmed, even if those stems are long, thick and woody, it's likely to be a bush rather than a tree. But, as with all black-and-white divisions, there is a grey place in between, where things aren't clear-cut. Common elder and hazel are naturally shrubby, while lots of trees can be coppiced – a management technique that results in multiple stems. Even something as reassuringly tree-like as a beech can be convinced to behave like a hedge.

The wild-growing 'tree' that I currently spend most time with has taken root on a thin scrap of earth beside the Regent's Canal in London. When our boat is moored here, this butterfly bush fills the view through one of the rear portholes, forming a partial screen between us and the towpath. Such a buffer is welcome when you live on a public waterway and people are inclined to treat your home as if it were street furniture. The buddleia spills out over the water at a thirty-degree angle like an unconvincing weeping willow, and birds, waterfowl and the occasional brown rat like to hide beneath its stoop. Over the course of a year, it will shelter coots, moorhens and mallards, Canada geese and swans, crows, gulls and wagtails, as well as our boat.

This butterfly bush has three main upright and trunk-like stems, each about as thick as my wrist, with brown bark that is vertically cracked. These stems are surrounded by multiple thinner, but equally woody shoots. It keeps its leaves through winter, and in the summer it zings. The electric-purple blooms are tiny, but cluster together tightly into spires that are large and eye-poppingly bright. Pollinators love them and, in turn, so do the canal's insect-eating birds and bats. While it doesn't recommend purposely planting buddleia anywhere other than in gardens, Butterfly Conservation says the butterfly bush easily lives up to its name. It always tops the list of plants most commonly used by butterflies in the charity's annual garden surveys, and it's become an important source of nectar as wildflower numbers have decreased.

The bright shimmer of painted butterfly wings on a sunny day is thrilling, as Vladimir Nabokov knew only too well, although he did rather like to catch and kill them. Writing about his love of butterfly-collecting for *The New Yorker* in 1948, the author and obsessive lepidopterist stated, 'I discovered in nature the nonutilitarian delights that I sought in art. Both were a form of magic, both were a game of intricate enchantment and deception.' When Nabokov stood among butterflies and their food plants he was in ecstasy, and behind that feeling lay something else that he couldn't quite explain, other than as 'a momentary vacuum into which rushes all that I love, a sense of oneness with sun and stone, a thrill of gratitude to whom it may concern'.

The canal-side buddleia flowers throughout summer, its spent spires gradually rusting to reddish-brown and setting seed. From autumn onwards, it could definitely be described as dishevelled. I see butterfly bushes like this one all over town. They appear as if from nowhere on land yet to be built on, or where whatever was there before has been torn down, but the next thing is yet to go up. It is the plant you'll glimpse from the top of a double-decker bus when you're afforded a rare peek behind hoardings, and the one you'll see growing rakishly out of some guttering, or spewing out of a broken chimney pot.

⁙

The butterfly bush was brought to the UK from China in the 1890s as a decorative plant for gardens. It escaped and became widespread as a weed in Britain after the Second World War, rushing through bomb sites, revelling in all the rubble. Buddleia thrives in places that are calcium-rich and well drained, and it's good at conserving water, so is able to cope well with drought. The human-made urban landscape mimics its natural one of rocky mountain tops and dry shingle. Buddleia is now seen growing in towns and cities across the UK, a plant of uncertain and disturbed land where the earth can be more like scree than soil. In the city, abandoned places like these can be important habitats. Within no time at all, forsaken ground will become overgrown and scrubby, as young woodland starts to take root. Left to its own devices, a wasteland will soon be able to host wildlife ranging from insects and invertebrates to birds and mammals. In these places, the butterfly bush can become a useful source of food and shelter for creatures passing through.

But because it is exotic, introduced and successful, buddleia is seen as a menace by some and is labelled invasive. Such plants challenge our ideas of what is, and isn't, natural. In an urban setting at the very least, scorning the non-native feels decidedly uncomfortable. Diversity of all kinds is what makes our cities vibrant and unique. In a paper on 'recombinant ecology', Ian Rotherham, Professor of Environmental Geography at Sheffield Hallam University, explains how the wild and the human-made have shuffled and combined to form cultural landscapes across all land types for centuries. He calls the mixing up of the native and the non-native within these places 'eco-fusion', and says the process has come to the fore as a result of global urbanization. In response, Rotherham has developed an elastic view of biodiversity: it's not fixed, but rather something that is 'shifting, drifting, fluxing'. This definition allows for mingling and mergers, for marriage and divorce and, I think, enables us to welcome characters like the butterfly bush into the understorey of the UK's urban forests.

ANOTHER URBAN UPSTART WORTH KNOWING

Tall, dark and hated, the Leyland cypress (*Cupressus* × *leylandii*) is common, but controversial. It's a robust evergreen with plumes of rubbery, scale-like leaves and a spire-like shape. It can be planted in packs to form a screening hedge, and is chosen for the privacy that its dense, dark foliage offers. But a lot of people experience it as a nutrient-grabbing light thief, a giant that strips the soil and condemns surrounding homes and gardens to perpetual dusk. It was the most frequently recorded urban tree in England in 2008, while the BBC claimed there were fifty-five million leylandii growing here in 2011, close to one per person. The tree is a hybrid that formed in the late 1880s when a Nootka cypress accidentally cross-fertilized with a Monterey cypress on a country estate in Wales. The two trees produced six offspring, and it's from these children that all Leyland cypresses descend. However, because those original offspring were infertile, every one of their many million descendants is a planted clone.

The cherries

There are hundreds of different types of cherry tree, and the *Prunus* genus of which it is a member also includes almond, peach, apricot and plum. Cherry fruits are both toothsome and rich in antioxidants, and fossil deposits suggest that we've eaten them for thousands of years. We also make use of cherry trees' decorative wood – it is strong and can be polished to a high gloss. The living trees have peeling bark with a satin sheen, and their leaves can turn warm sunset shades in autumn. But, as important harbingers of spring, it's their blowsy blossom that is celebrated most.

WILD CHERRY
Prunus avium

'*Avium*' probably refers to the fact that, like us, birds love cherries. In Scotland, the wild cherry tree is sometimes also known as '*gean*', and in Highland folklore encountering one was considered auspicious and fateful.

Shape is small, stout, rounded but spiky. (Fig. 16)

Leaves are oval, large and limp with toothed edges. (Fig. 17)

Bark is reddish, peeling and shiny, horizontally striped, becoming craggy with age.

Flowers are large and white, cup-shaped, opening ahead of the leaves in spring. (Fig. 18)

Fruit are bright red and bitter, small and round.

Found in urban parkland and woods, in gardens and along city streets.

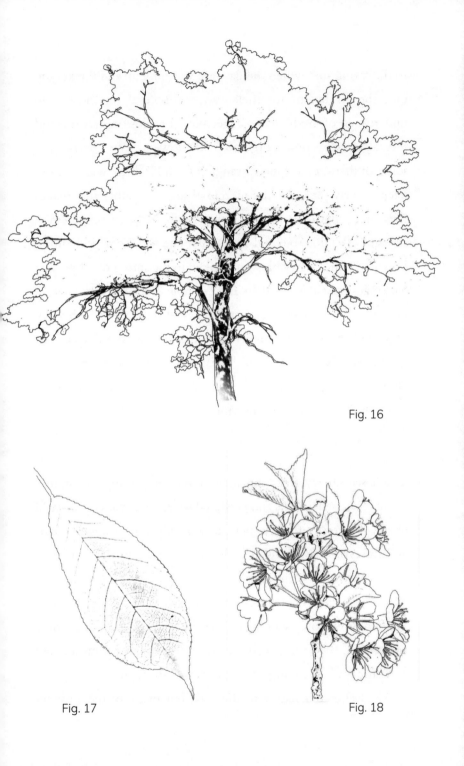

Fig. 16

Fig. 17

Fig. 18

In the springtime, when the days are warming up and thickening out, the air begins to smell new, with floral top notes and undertones of fresh, leafy vegetable. It's blossom season and several trees become gorgeous with flowers. The cherries are some of them, their blooms ranging from brightest white to the deepest dirty pink. It's the mercurial spring weather that makes these trees appealing, backlit as they often are by a strengthening sun and a sky that rolls and seethes like the sea. Remarking upon how lavish the cherry blossom looked in the spring of 1948, Vita Sackville-West described in *Let Us Now Praise Famous Gardens* how the 'heavy whiteness' was deepened by a 'pewter-grey sky of storm', how well matched the 'dazzling blossom' was with the 'peculiarly lurid heaven'. Gleams of light framed the storm clouds, and every now and then a lance of pure gold broke through. The effect was dramatic.

::::

You'll see cherry trees throughout the city, lining up prettily along residential streets and clustered together in parks. The wild cherry flowers before its new leaves fully unfurl after winter, and the ivory blooms sit heavily on twiggy, still-bare branches. It's a celebrated spring awakening, although from a distance a blossom-covered cherry tree can look as if it's caked with snow. Sudden downpours will bruise the flowers, and eventually they are cast off. Browning petals lie on lawns and pavements like old confetti, as if a wedding party had passed through.

Wild cherry is native to the UK, but many of the varieties

you'll see around town originally hail from China or Japan. And although it's their blossom for which they are best known and loved, the trees also have decorative bark, which I enjoy just as much. Rich shades of ruby or copper, cherry bark is metal-smooth, polished and peeling, the burnished skin being slowly shed in thin horizontal strips that curl up tightly against the trunk. The bark is also marked with 'lenticels', small raised pores that are common to most plants. These lentil-sized openings allow gaseous exchange to take place, enabling the tree to breathe. They are particularly noticeable on the cherry, where – confusingly – they don't look like lentils at all, but instead take the shape of black bands that encircle the trunk.

Cherry leaves, meanwhile, are large and limp, hanging floppily on the branch. Oval-shaped, they have pointed ends and serrated edges, with sharp but shallow teeth. Green most of the time, a cherry tree's leaves can be glorious in autumn, flushing coral-pink and apricot, as well as burgundy and scarlet. If you get up close to one and flip it over, you should be able to see two small but prominent red bumps where the leaf meets the stem. These are extrafloral nectaries, glands from which the tree secretes a sugary nectar in order to attract garden ants, which in turn deter other, more destructive, leaf-eating insects. Should a foraging ant encounter a caterpillar, say, as it journeys about the cherry's foliage in search of sugar, it will act aggressively towards it, fending the caterpillar off or even eating it.

Many plants and animals work together like this, their lives interconnected or interdependent. In *Directives for New*

Life, Dane Rudhyar describes how the Earth is an intricately organized system of activities – an 'organic planetary whole' – with species from all the life-kingdoms dependent on each other for survival, and dependent on the wider environment too, be that oceanic or atmospheric currents or the protective ionosphere. He argues that humankind is as much a part of this planetary whole as the ants and the plants, that all of us are connected. In his book *Biophilia*, published about a decade later in 1984, the naturalist E. O. Wilson describes an expedition that he made to Bernhardsdorp in Surinam as a young man, in search of new species of ants. Contemplating the rainforest, he describes it as an ocean, and himself as a diver: 'I knew that all around me bits and pieces, the individual organisms and their populations, were working with extreme precision.' He notes that some of the species are locked together so intricately that to lose one would mean losing the other. Wondering where the reverberations would end, should a single species go extinct, he concludes, 'It is enough to work on the assumption that all of the details matter in the end, in some unknown but vital way.' Although neither the cherry tree nor the garden ant is dependent on the other for its ultimate survival, their symbiotic relationship – or 'protocooperation' – is of mutual benefit. The ant offers the tree protection, and in exchange the ant gets food that the cherry can afford to give up. Without each other, the world for both would be a less hospitable place.

::::

Loved in the UK, the Japanese flowering cherry is of huge cultural significance in its home country. Each year's blossoming is a key moment in Japan's calendar, and many traditions hinge around the event, including '*hanami*', which involves picnicking and singing under the blooming cherry trees. That, in turn, now sits alongside the year-round tradition of forest bathing, or '*shinrin-yoku*'. A term coined in the 1980s, this simply involves taking in the forest atmosphere in a leisurely, aimless manner, and recognizes just how soothing trees can be for the spirit. More widely, the flowering cherry has become synonymous with the global peace movement and the fight for a nuclear-free world. When a peace park and peace boulevard were designed and planted in the Japanese city of Hiroshima in the 1950s, the cherry was a focal point, chosen as a symbol as much as a plant. In a paper called 'Planting "Post-Conflict" Landscapes: Urban Trees in Peacebuilding and Reconstruction', academic Mark Johnston explains that the regeneration of Hiroshima after the Second World War 'forged the long-standing peace iconography that persists to this day', and nowhere is this more apparent than in the 'symbolic weight of the Japanese cherry tree'.

On a recent lunchtime walk I discovered a mature cherry growing in Tavistock Square in Bloomsbury, close to where I work. In a leafy place, this tree stood out. A small plaque on short stilts explained that it had been planted in 1967 to commemorate the victims of the atomic bombings in Hiroshima. Tree-planting *in memoriam* like this is popular throughout the UK and beyond – it can be a ritualistic, therapeutic act that looks forward as well as back. As the author and environmentalist Rachel Carson wrote in *The Sense of Wonder*, 'There is something infinitely healing in the repeated refrains of nature – the assurance that dawn comes after night and spring after winter.' Paying close attention to a tree as it cycles through the seasons can give you a reassuring sense of renewal and growth.

The Tavistock cherry itself is comparatively small – the square's other trees tower over it – but it's large and rather gnarled for a cherry. I'd guess it's about sixty or seventy years old. It has a squat, barrel-shaped trunk, with five large limbs radiating up and out from the top of it like five fat fingers, each knuckle at about shoulder-height. These fingers spread wide, and the upper branches they support have an elegantly arching shape, giving the tree the silhouette of an open umbrella. There might once have been a sixth finger, but all that's left is a lumpen scar marking the site of a long-ago battle with a tree surgeon or the wind. At first glance, the tree's bark appears dark brown, but the longer I look, the more purple-red it becomes. It has that classic cherry-tree sheen and is striped with horizontal bands, but it also has large patches of unusually rough skin around the base. The well-worn ground beneath the tree roils with roots.

The first time I met this tree, it was bare of flowers and foliage. I decide to visit it regularly as winter turns into spring, to watch it blossom and come back into leaf, and to see if I can find something of what Carson was describing. My visits start in early February and are brief, because of the weather. However, by the end of the month I've got into a routine of visiting once a week during lunch breaks from work. Despite snow and gale-force winds, the tree has leaf buds, although these don't open for several weeks. Over time I begin to notice more about the tree, including just how warty its skin is, and how pronounced its lenticels are, which look quite orange in the early spring light. I watch over the weeks as the dark, reddish-brown leaf buds gradually swell and become green. These are eventually joined by flower buds, which are tiny, round and red, hanging on long stalks. By the end of April the cherry is smothered in sugary-pink blossom, and the tree seems to stoop slightly under the extra weight. The coppery new leaves it was sporting the week before have disappeared from sight, and the branches that arch out over the footpath form a floral canopy for people to sit beneath. Petals float on the breeze. Up close, the blossom is clustered into large bunches, the shape, size and colour of candy floss.

And then, and seemingly just like that, most of the Tavistock cherry's blossom has fallen – its moment of glory was brief, spanning a fortnight at most. The footpath and lawn surrounding it are pinkish-brown with spent petals. The tree's leaves are back in view, now large, green and fresh. I think back over the last few weeks. Winter has turned into spring, reasserted itself savagely, but eventually lost out, as I always knew it would. A plan to visit regularly, which I felt reluctant about at first, has now become a weekly habit, a moment of calm amid a whirlwind of work and real life. Paying attention like this means I do have a stronger sense of what Rachel Carson was describing, and something of what Dane Rudhyar and E. O. Wilson were too. This is partly because I've found out that I'm pregnant – the cherry tree and I have been blooming in unison, our lifecycles briefly synced. Visiting on a hot day in May, I lie back in its gauzy shade to watch the ants. I fold my hands over my leavened belly as my baby turns somersaults inside, and I let my changing body be cradled by the tree's roots and the warm earth.

ANOTHER FLOWERING FRUIT WORTH KNOWING

One of the sylvan city's smallest members – attaining a height of no more than ten metres, and doing so in a twisting, turning sort of way – the crab apple makes up for what it lacks in grandeur with bounteous flowers and fruit. The wild crab (*Malus sylvestris*) is shrubby, sometimes thorny. Like all apple trees, it has scaly bark that cracks into distinctive square plates. Large white flowers are followed by cherry-sized fruits that birds love, and which foragers can boil and sweeten into jellies and jams. There are many ornamental crab-apple varieties, including weeping ones that are cultivated for their melancholy slouch. The crab apple is also a parent of the domestic apple tree, of which there are more than 7,500 different varieties, producing fruits that can be eaten raw or cooked, and pressed into cider and juice.

The apple tree is famous for the role it plays in both the Christian creation myth and the legend of how gravity was discovered. The Bible isn't specific about what the forbidden fruit growing on the tree of the knowledge of good and evil was, but it's depicted as an apple in western Europe. This is possibly because the Latin words for 'apple' and 'evil' – *malus* – are the same. Meanwhile, it's unclear whether the story that Isaac Newton came up with the theory of gravity after an apple fell from a tree and hit him on the head is true, or whether it was simply a useful metaphor that he embellished over time.

The elders

The elders tend to be shrubby plants with strong-smelling clusters of flowers in spring, followed by dark berry-shaped fruits in summer. There is plenty of old folklore surrounding these trees, including that they were guarded by the Elder Mother, from whom you must ask permission before taking the tree's wood, else she'd have her revenge. It was rumoured that if you did burn elder, you would see the Devil, but if you chose to plant it close to home, it would keep the Devil away. Today, people are more worried about keeping up appearances than about courting tree spirits. There are several ornamental elder cultivars on the market, grown in gardens for their attractive foliage, flowers and fruits.

COMMON ELDER
Sambucus nigra

'Elder' derives from the Anglo-Saxon '*aeld*', meaning fire, probably because the tree's hollow stems were once used as bellows to make fires roar; '*nigra*' means dark, likely in reference to the colour of elderberries.

Shape is shrubby and irregular; new poles shoot straight up, then hook over at the top. (Fig. 19)

Leaves are compound, with toothed leaflets growing in opposite pairs from each leaf stalk. (Fig. 20)

Bark is pale and warty when young, becoming browner and deeply furrowed with age.

Flowers are hermaphrodite, cream-coloured and clustered, with an unpleasant scent. (Fig. 21)

Fruit are small, pitch-black berries, tightly packed on red stems.

Found in scrubby in-between spaces, edge-lands, derelict or disturbed ground.

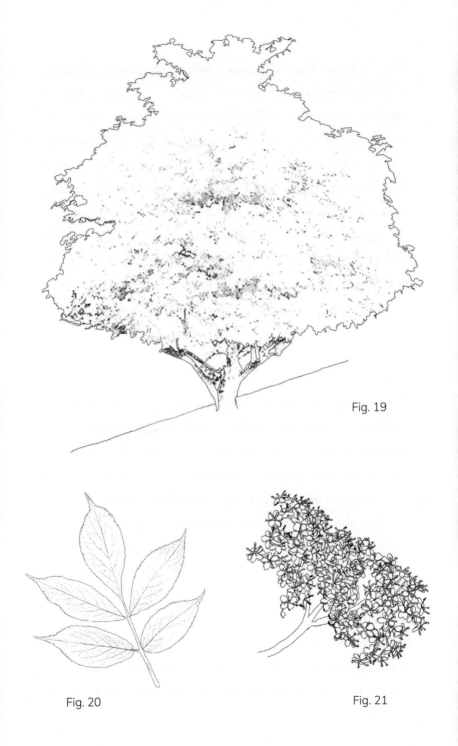

Fig. 19

Fig. 20

Fig. 21

The elder, a bit like the butterfly bush, is a tree of those scrubby, in-between spaces that exist in all cities. It's in the habit of growing on the edges of things, often where it's not supposed to, and is sometimes accused of being a weed. The one I know best is sandwiched between a road bridge and a sewage pipe, but you might spot one sprouting up on a rubbly patch behind buildings, in a railway siding, a car park or your neighbour's neglected back yard. It's one of the first trees to come back into leaf after winter, and by spring it's covered with cheerful, strong-smelling flowers. In summer those dense cream blooms will sun-ripen into bunches of black berries that droop on crimson stems.

⁞⁞⁞

As I started to find out more about elder, I quickly learned that it's a tree revered by those who study and practise herbal medicine – people like Vicky Chown and Kim Walker. They founded the Handmade Apothecary after meeting at university, and have made it their mission to teach people about the health-giving benefits of urban trees and plants. I'm introduced to them in a roundabout way, and although I'm eager to talk to them, I'm not sure they'll want to be grilled by me about elder. But the prospect seems to appeal, and they suggest that I pay them a visit at their current base in Queen's Wood, north London.

I decide to travel there by Tube rather than bike, as my destination sits at the top of a steep hill. It's a decision I quickly regret. There's something about the Northern Line that makes it more oppressive than other Underground routes, perhaps because it's one of the network's deep-level lines – 58.5 metres below street level at its deepest point in Hampstead – or maybe because it's so airless. In 2002, an investigation by scientists at University College London into air quality on the Tube revealed that it was seventy-three times worse than above ground, and the Northern Line was worst of all: allegedly, spending twenty minutes on it had the same effect as smoking a cigarette. Whatever the cause, my journey from Old Street to Highgate leaves me sweating and queasy. The walk to the wood is along a busy rush-hour road, and it's a relief finally to get inside among the trees. The light immediately mottles. The traffic noise dips and is soon muffled by leaves. The sun that can penetrate illuminates clouds of gnats and slow-floating motes. The change of scene is soothing, and I can feel my thick head starting to thin out.

The community garden where Vicky has been working all day is on the rim of the wood, and I can see her in there from afar, winding up a long hose. She looks worn-out, but the moment she spots me, she brightens and welcomes me in. Vicky explains that it's been a volunteering day in the garden, busy with people of all ages and abilities, and so quite intense. The garden is quiet now – a small space, but one full of flowers, herbs and trees, including an elder on its far edge. Vicky finishes winding the hose back onto its reel and then sits with me at a picnic bench.

A car rolls up and Kim steps out. She's come from Kew, where she works in the economic botany department. The women explain that they set up the Handmade Apothecary as a way to encourage people to enjoy their local green spaces and connect with nature. Education is what motivates them most of all. Everything they do – the guided walks, the workshops, the column in the local newspaper – is designed to teach people about the plants growing all around us, and how they can be used at home. Vicky and Kim seem to have developed a relationship with the city that's different from most people's – they see it as a well-stocked larder, one with the power to heal.

I ask about the medicinal uses for elder, and what they think the tree's distinguishing features are. Their response is to invite me to spend some time standing under one, insisting that identifying plants is about meeting them in person. And it's not just about using your eyes, they say; you should also smell and touch what you see.

The community garden's elder is characteristically shrubby, with branches low down on the trunk as well as high up. It has a central stem with lots of slender poles growing around it. These shoot straight up and then hook over at the top, like walking sticks. I sweep my hands over its bronzed, warty young bark, then rake my hands through the foliage, feeling how soft the leaves are, and discovering how pungent they smell when crushed. I learn that they can be used externally as an insect repellent, or infused in massage oil to ease muscle ache, bruises and sprains.

It may be acceptable to gently manhandle an elder like this, in order to get to know it better, but folklore warns that to cut it down would be bad luck. Vicky and Kim suggest this cautionary tale came about for good reason – the intention could well have been to stop people destroying a source of food and medicine, as well as to prevent physical harm. The elder's leaves and bark contain cyanogenic glycosides, which break down to form cyanide, and if you eat either you'll be ill. Purging was a widespread practice in the past, and people often thought a medicine's efficacy lay in its ability to void the human body. *The Anatomie of the Elder*, first published in the 1630s, is devoted to the tree's medicinal uses, including its role as a purgative. There's an old saying which advises that if you strip elder bark upwards, it will make you vomit; if you strip it downwards, it will make you shit.

For contemporary medical herbalists, however, it's elderflowers and elderberries that are important. Spring blossom can be picked and dried, then made into tinctures and teas, as well as cordial and champagne, all of which are good for treating hay fever, colds and flu. Elderflowers contain flavonoids, fatty acids and minerals, especially potassium, among other phytochemicals, and are anti-catarrhal, anti-inflammatory and immunostimulant. Despite their powers, the fresh flowers smell revolting. Vicky and Kim describe it as a scent somewhere between cat urine and death, and yet pollinating insects find it irresistible. I'm keen to know if supermarket elderflower cordial has any medicinal value. The answer, Vicky tells me, is yes – probably – as long as it is made from real elderflowers and not from artificial flavouring. The next time I feel a cold coming on, I'm instructed to drink elderflower cordial diluted with hot water and go straight to bed.

Elderberries follow the flowers in summer. They can be

harvested and then simmered to make tea, cooked into pies or dried and used like raisins. They are anti-viral and immune-boosting and, like a lot of dark fruits, are generally good for the health of the veins. The Handmade Apothecary produces an elder elixir, which Vicky swears by. She argues that, if we're willing to open our minds to the traditions of the past, we'll find that a lot of them still have relevance and value. Back then, people were looking to plants for solutions for short-term, acute conditions. Today we have conventional medicine synthesized in laboratories for dealing with such problems, but herbal medicine can still be useful. It's about maintaining good health as much as it is about treating illness, and a lot of herbal medicines are also vitamin-rich foodstuffs.

:::::

Where Vicky is salt of the earth, Kim is crisper and more analytical. Her interest in botany started in childhood, and from a young age she wanted to know what plants were called. I ask her whether we need to know the names of things in order to appreciate them. Is knowing that an elder is an elder – that it is *Sambucus nigra* – really necessary?

I ask the question because deciding to call something by its name, something that might seem on the surface like a straightforward exercise in intimacy, isn't necessarily as simple as that. The botanist and zoologist Carl Linnaeus, who formalized the modern convention of naming organisms, wrote in *Philosophia Botanica* in 1751, 'If you do not know the name of things, the knowledge is lost too.' But there's no doubt that taxonomy – systematically classifying the natural world – says as much about the human doing the naming as it is does about the thing they are trying to describe. In his essay 'Why Look at Animals?', art critic John Berger suggests that what we know about the non-human world is 'an index of our power', and thus 'an index of what separates us'. He says that the more we choose to know about other living things, the further away they become. Author John Fowles writes about this specifically in relation to plants, in his book *The Tree*. He argues that even a basic knowledge of flowers or trees 'destroys or curtails certain possibilities of seeing'. If we truly want to be at one with the trees, is it actually better to know nothing about them, other than what we have witnessed first-hand?

Kim doesn't think so. While experiencing a plant in person is important, knowing its name is too, for two reasons. First, in terms of herbalism, misidentification could lead to poisoning. When we meet a tree, and through sight, touch and smell are able to establish that it's an elder, we can then access information about it that advises us which of its parts it is, and is not, wise to eat. Botanical names provide an international language that botanists the world over, whatever their mother tongue, can understand. Second, once you know that a tree is an elder, that name is also a doorway. Knowing it, you're in a position to find out what has already been discovered and what questions are yet to be asked. A name, and the story that inevitably comes with it, invites you to get more involved. In *The Songs of Trees*, biologist

David George Haskell argues that urban trees that exist within the 'human social network' have much better survival rates than those that remain anonymous: 'A street tree that is granted personhood and membership, one that is noticed, loved, and given identity and history, lives longer than a municipal object, arriving with no context and living with no collaborators.'

Formal knowledge about the natural world is on the wane – from words like 'acorn', 'bramble' and 'catkin' being dropped from the *Oxford Junior Dictionary*, to the death of the undergraduate botany degree in Britain – yet we need nature now as much as we always did. We need it for all the practical things it offers, including food and medicine, and we need it for our inner lives too. When E. O. Wilson explored the concept of 'biophilia' in his book of the same name, he described it as 'the urge to affiliate with other forms of life'. It's an urge that I definitely have. If most of us now live in urban areas – as more than half of the world's population does – we need to be able to affiliate in a city setting as much as anywhere else.

Kim and Vicky are keen to point out that their city-centric foraging for herbs isn't just about the pursuit of good physical health; it's about good mental health too. They believe that simply being in nature has a healing effect, and they're not alone in thinking this, nor is it a new idea. In *The Consolations of Philosophy*, specifically in his 'Consolation for Frustration', Alain de Botton describes the anxiety-ridden years experienced by the stoic Seneca, who had the misfortune of working for the tyrannical Roman emperor Nero. With his position precarious until his untimely death at Nero's command in 65 CE, Seneca devoted himself to philosophy and studying the natural world. Botton explains that Seneca gained 'immense relief from the spectacle of nature – perhaps because in mighty natural phenomena lie reminders of all that we are powerless to change ... It is apparent from the heedless pounding of the oceans or the flight of comets across the night sky that there are forces entirely indifferent to our desires.' Connecting with nature can be freeing, and its disinterest in our worries permits us to let them go, at least for a while. On the flip side, disconnecting from nature can make us depressed: American author Richard Louv coined the term 'nature deficit disorder' to describe just how bad it is for our health.

I love being freed from myself through trees. My city is in constant flux, and if I don't keep moving, I won't keep up. There's something about trees' slow steadiness that makes them perfect company in the face of this. As E. O. Wilson observed, humanity isn't exalted because we're above other living things, but because 'knowing them well elevates the very concept of life'. It gives life meaning. Knowing a tree by name – knowing an elder is an elder – is an important first step.

OTHER TREES CELEBRATED BY HERBALISTS

After elder, the lime is one of the trees most loved by medical herbalists. It's cherished for its relaxing and calming effects, especially in France, where lime-flower tea is a popular drink. It's a delicate brew with a honey-like taste, into which you could dip a madeleine in homage to Marcel Proust. The pine tree is also of great value to herbalists as the source of an aromatic, antiseptic essential oil that can be added to a bath to relieve muscle tension and unblock sinuses.

The elms

Elms grow as street, garden and parkland trees as well as in the wild. They're tolerant of sea spray and are a popular planting choice along coasts. Before metal was widely available, many towns' and cities' water mains were made from elm wood, which doesn't rot when wet. The Science Museum has part of an elm water pipe in its collection, dating from fifteenth- or sixteenth-century London. There are many types of elm tree – up to sixty different species – but all of them produce a tiny lentil-like fruit that's surrounded by a leafy, disc-shaped wing. The elms also all have fuzzy, lopsided leaves with ragged edges, arranged alternately along the branch.

ENGLISH ELM

Ulmus minor

The English elm is also known as the field elm, and both names hint at the fact that this was once a tree commonly found growing on farmland in England, especially in the Midlands and the south.

Shape is tall, stately, with a dense, drooping canopy. (Fig. 22)

Leaves are deeply toothed, dark green and roundish, fuzzily rough to the touch. (Fig. 23)

Bark is brown, cracked and vertically ridged, becoming nobbled.

Flowers are hermaphrodite, reddish and tiny, clustered together into spiky tufts. (Fig. 24)

Fruit is a small seed enclosed inside a flimsy pale-green disc.

Found in parks, streets and gardens, especially in Brighton and Hove.

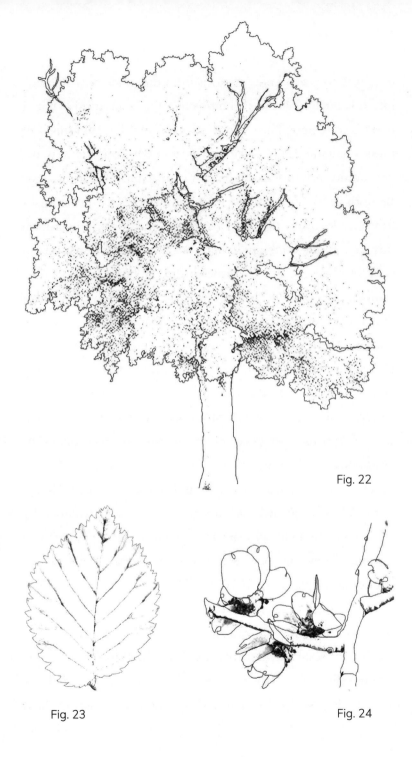

Fig. 22

Fig. 23

Fig. 24

One way to get to know a tree is from the inside out. Stepping into this English elm was an intimate act, and an invasive one. I don't belong here, but I like it. It's cool and dim, and smells of mushroom and damp. I like how cocooned I feel, and how the city outside seems less insistent. It's quiet but the elm is busy. Beneath its bark are tubes that are transporting self-made sugars from the leaves to the branches, trunk and roots. Underneath this 'bast' is the 'cambium', which is a layer of tissue that creates cells for plant growth. Underneath the cambium is wood. The cambium produces both bast and wood. The newest wood is called 'sapwood', and it contains vessels that distribute water and nutrients from the roots throughout the tree. After fifteen to twenty years those vessels will block and become 'heartwood', with new sapwood taking its place. It's the outer layers that dispense the essential things that keep the tree alive, which is why an elm like this one, almost entirely hollowed out of its heartwood, can continue to live.

This hollow tree is in Brighton, a coastal city that's home to the UK's National Collection of elms — a status awarded by the conservation charity Plant Heritage that means the host will document, develop and preserve a comprehensive collection of one group of plants. In 2016, UNESCO designated the area a World Biosphere Reserve, partly due to its elms. Once you open your eyes to them, you realize they're everywhere and, just as much as the seafront, these trees are part of Brighton's personality. I've travelled here with my friend Clare and we've started our journey through the city's forest in Preston Park, where stand a venerable pair known as 'the twins'. These huge trees are more than 400 years old and are thought to be the oldest elms in Europe. They're probably the overgrown remnants of an old elm hedge. They're pruned regularly to keep the weight of their canopies low and, from a distance, they look almost youthful, certainly robust, neatly shaped and well kept. Up close, you feel the full force of their years. Their grey-brown rhino skin is burred and bulging, they're covered in gargoyle-like bosses, and both are as hollow as drainpipes. One – the tree we've already met – has an inviting crack in it.

As soon as we arrive, Clare slips inside the elm – the crack is big enough for an adult to enter easily – and doesn't come out for some time. As I wait my turn, wondering what secrets she's found inside, I circle the tree, touching its deeply grooved bark and fingering its fuzzy leaves. Once, on Hampstead Heath, I found a key hidden inside a hollow tree. It became the source of much speculation. The Preston Park twins, like many old elms, are home to a colony of rare white-letter hairstreak butterflies, a species that is completely dependent on elm trees for its food. I look up, hopeful. The butterflies live right at the top of the tree, making them difficult to spot.

Clare re-emerges, I take my turn inside and then we walk over to have a look at the other twin. It's not possible to get inside this one without crawling, which we decide against. This elm is even more nobbled than the other, covered in calluses and sporting an enormous warty protrusion on one side. It's a beast. We picnic with the twins in view, and tie ourselves in knots thinking about what being alive for four centuries could possibly be like. These two trees have changed dramatically, if slowly, over that time, gradually growing from saplings into hedge fellows and now stately individuals, buffeted by the weather and human hands into their current characterful shapes. But they've also been rooted to a single spot. Static, stoical, while the human world around them has ripped itself apart and re-formed, over and over – their long lives have encompassed a civil war, the unification of Scotland and England, the Industrial Revolution, two world wars, the founding of the NHS, Brexit.

::::

There are around 17,000 elms in Brighton and Hove. This number isn't just impressive, it's incredible, given the wider context. In the 1970s, a virulent elm disease in the form of an aggressive fungus swept through Britain, killing an estimated twenty-five million trees, and all but wiping out the English elm within a single cruel decade. It first arrived on British shores in some imported elm logs and was quickly spread by bark beetles. The English elm tends to reproduce by suckering, an asexual way of regenerating from a stem or root, meaning that an elm's offspring are clones rather than genetically distinct, which makes them vulnerable to disease. It's one of the reasons why the fungus ascent was so swift.

English elms were imposing trees, with a silhouette ominously said to resemble a mushroom cloud. While it still exists in a shrubby, short-lived form today, what was once a widespread and distinctive-looking tree is now rare. W. G. Sebald describes the loss of six elm trees from his Norfolk garden in *The Rings of Saturn*: they 'withered away in June 1978, just a few weeks after they unfolded their marvellous light green foliage for the last time'. Another, solitary elm – 'one of the most perfect trees I had ever seen' – was 100 feet tall and 'filled an immense space' in a field close to Sebald's house. Although it was in seemingly good health, within a fortnight its leaves had browned and curled and were 'dust before autumn came', the disease having caused the tree's capillaries to tighten and it to die of thirst. For those who lived through it, tree enthusiast or not, the visual impact of elm disease on the landscape was dramatic.

It is in Brighton that one can learn more about what's been lost. Although without significant tree cover before the 1800s, the area has long since been one dominated by elms, not least because local aristocrats liked planting them. The elm was a popular choice because it was one of the few large trees that could thrive in Brighton and Hove's chalky soil. In 1845, the third earl of Chichester gifted 1,000 elms to an area known as The Level, once common land, today a landscaped urban park. A hundred years later, Brighton was blessed with a parks and gardens team that sourced and planted a number of elm varieties and cultivars.

Salty sea air and the barrier formed by the South Downs National Park, a firebreak of open, largely treeless grassland, helped shield Brighton and Hove from elm disease's worst ravages, while disease management was taken seriously from day one, and continues to be today. Since the 1970s there has been a policy of pruning or felling infected and unhealthy trees to stop the disease spreading. Brighton's parks staff are trained to spot the symptoms, the city has a dedicated elm-disease inspector, and refuse collectors have even been recruited to the cause, providing extra eyes on the ground.

As Clare and I continue our journey through Brighton, we come across some diseased elms at The Level, including the stump of one that has already been cut down. The still-standing trees are large, with bright-yellow posters pinned to their trunks and the bark around their bases shorn off. The posters encourage people to contact the council arboriculture team to have their elm trees and logs inspected for free. Behind the unwell elms are some healthy trees, one of which has a large collection of shoes hanging from its branches. Why people throw footwear into trees, and indeed over power lines, remains mysterious, but it's a popular and widespread pastime. There's a map on the Roadside America website that pinpoints where some of the United States' most spectacular shoe trees are, while *The Daily Telegraph* and the *Daily Mail* have both reported on a project that aimed to solve the mystery of an ash tree that was completely covered in shoes alongside the A40 in Buckinghamshire, somewhere between High Wycombe and Stokenchurch. Theories ranged from pagan fertility ritual to preparation for an alien landing, but the investigation was ultimately fruitless.

Next we push our bikes through the steep rainbow streets of Kemp Town and then roll down into Queens Park and, as we do, we realize that spending time with the twins and on The

Level means we're already becoming adept at identifying elms. We wheel through the park, easily picking out the elms from the other trees, noting their vertically ridged bark, which makes Clare think of ropes, and their toothed leaves, which are rough to the touch and have a beaky tip. On the way to the Royal Pavilion Gardens we discover that elms grow as street trees here as well as in parks.

It is at the Pavilion that we seek out the English elm known locally as the 'Brace Tree'. It was planted in the 1780s and has had a tough life. It's currently cramped on the side of a busy tourist trail through the park, mostly ignored by the many passers-by. It's as gnarled and hollowed-out as the Preston Park twins, but looks a lot less comfortable in its dotage. Two wide metal bands have been clamped around its trunk. They've been in place for decades and have become integrated into the bark, as if the tree were attempting to swallow them up. Human-sized cracks have opened in the trunk, and subsequently have been covered with wire mesh to discourage people from clambering in or using the tree as a bin. The bands may be supportive and the mesh protective, but they make the tree look shackled and caged.

This afternoon the Brace Tree is guarded by a man with wide eyes, a pea-green beard and a walking stick with two bicycle bells attached to it. He seems surprised but pleased by our interest in the tree, and dings his bells triumphantly. The green man looks so much like a goblin or tree spirit that it feels like I must have magicked him up, and I find myself catching Clare's eye to make sure she sees him, too. He dings the bells again, as if to confirm that he exists. I look up into the tree's dark, sun-punched canopy. At first it seems as if it, too, is full of tossed trainers, but then my eyes adjust and I see the black clumps are in fact roosting pigeons. The elm is forlorn, although I could be projecting my own weariness onto it – a calm day is ending in a crowded part of Brighton. Well over 200 years old, the Brace Tree appears emblematic of the toilsome course that life can take. But its beleaguered looks don't stop it seeming tough, and it is loved – by the people who have cared for it over those two centuries, encircling it with mesh and metal rather than seeing it misused or collapse; by the birds that choose it as a safe place to rest; by the man with the pea-green beard; and now by us.

ANOTHER ELM WORTH KNOWING

The wild-growing wych elm (*Ulmus glabra*) is found in woodlands, especially in Scotland, but it's sometimes planted, too. Its toothy leaves are large and characteristically fuzzy, while the bark is grey becoming brownish, forming cracks, bosses and furrows with age. This produces a wood with a so-called 'burr grain', characterized by irregular markings. The ornamental weeping form is sometimes found in urban parks and botanic gardens. 'Wych' derives from '*wice*', an Old English word meaning bendable or pliant, and which also gives us the words 'wicker' and 'weak'.

The figs

Part of the mulberry family, there are thought to be hundreds of different types of fig tree. Most grow in warm or tropical climes. Fig flowers are concealed in the centre of its fruit, and fertilization depends on a symbiotic relationship with specialized fig-wasps. Fossil evidence suggests that fig trees were one of the first food plants ever cultivated by humans.

COMMON FIG
Ficus carica

The classical Greek origin of the word 'sycophant' has an interesting connection with the fig – according to author Robin Wakefield, '*sykophantes*' means 'tale-teller about figs', and it was used to denounce someone who ingratiated themselves with the Athenian authorities by reporting illegal fig-smuggling.

Shape is short and lumpish, with low-spreading, twisting branches. (Fig. 25)

Leaves are dark green, large and leathery, with three or five deep lobes. (Fig. 26)

Bark is pale grey, smooth, but with handsome nobbles.

Flowers are hidden inside the fruit.

Fruit is large and fleshy, green, purple or brown. (Fig. 27)

Found in sheltered parks and gardens, and along once-warm rivers in Sheffield.

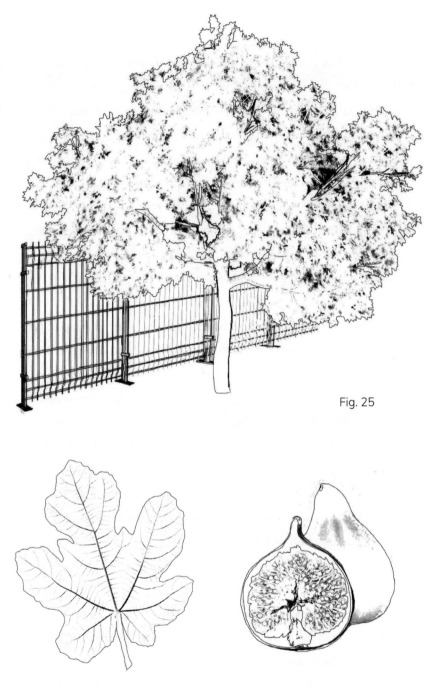

Fig. 25

Fig. 26

Fig. 27

In a world of giants, the fig tree is relatively diminutive, although it can live for hundreds of years. Growing no more than ten metres tall, it can be called a shrub as much as a tree. It has a domed, low and wide-spreading crown, with branches that twist and turn, and dark leaves that are large and leather-like – foliage big enough to clothe a freshly fallen Adam and Eve. Many different cultivars exist and it's regularly planted as an ornamental. Knowing that the common fig is a relative of the rubber plant – perhaps there's one collecting dust somewhere at home? – might help you recognize it in the wild. Their leaves aren't the same shape, but they're a similar texture.

Figs favour and flourish in warm climates. They are one of our most common rainforest plants and an important source of food for forest fruit-eaters: a single rainforest fig tree can produce more than 100,000 fruits. Wild figs have co-evolved with fig-wasps to form an incredible, mutualistic bond. The tree secretly flowers in autumn, with the blooms enclosed inside its fruit. The fig-wasp tunnels into the fruit, pollinating the almost impossible-to-reach flowers and enabling the tree to reproduce, while, in return, the fruit provides the fig-wasp with a safe nest to lay its eggs, and food for its young when they hatch. There are several hundred varieties of fig tree and each has its own corresponding fig-wasp.

The fig's range isn't limited to rainforests – it's found in urban jungles too. An early city tree that was shown some serious respect was a revered fig named 'Ruminalis'. It grew in ancient Rome's forum, at the heart of the city, where it was worshipped through the ages and its health was a matter of public concern. In *The Golden*

Bough, first published in 1890, James George Frazer describes how 'the withering of its trunk was enough to spread consternation throughout the city'. The naturalist Pliny the Elder, who lived from 23 to 79 CE, also wrote about this sacred tree, explaining that it memorialized the legendary fig under which the founders of Rome – Romulus and Remus – were nursed by a she-wolf.

::::

The fig trees found in the UK aren't native, and when and where they occur is usually due to human intervention, purposeful or otherwise. The wild-growing urban fig is therefore an uncommon delight in Britain, and individuals are famous among tree-lovers. The encyclopaedic *Flora Britannica* highlights the fig growing out of the stonework of Bristol Temple Meads station and the Dalmarnock fig of Glasgow, found on the River Clyde, while whole articles have been published in the *Yorkshire Post* about Leeds' fig trees. There's a gnarled fig I know growing on a back street in Islington that has been officially declared a 'Great Tree of London'. It's so old and crooked that its low, long-reaching branches are being held up by A-shaped metal splints. In winter, its bulging trunk looks like the solidified drips of wax that build up around an empty wine-bottle candlestick.

But it is in Sheffield that you will find a whole forest of figs growing wild. They thrive along a chilly urban waterway, which is remarkable, considering the tree's preference for balmy weather. Ecologist Oliver Gilbert conducted extensive research into his city's surprising population of wild figs in the 1980s, concluding that it was a direct result of the city's industrialization, and specifically of the impact of the steel industry on the temperature of the River Don. In his book *The Ecology of Urban Habitats*, published in 1989, Gilbert noted that there were thirty to forty wild figs growing along the waterway, none of which were young. He deduced that the trees had established themselves when manufacturing was at its height. Back then, river water was used for cooling and the Don ran at a constant twenty degrees Celsius as a result. Sewage was also flowing into the river. A number of fig seeds found in the sewage germinated along the riverbank, fooled by the warm water into thinking they were in the Med. My favourite explanation for the presence of the seeds is local people's partiality for fig biscuits.

I want to see these figs for myself, so I travel to Sheffield to find them. They're growing just out of town in the vicinity of Hadfield Weir. I'm imagining somewhere sleepy and idyllic, but it turns out the weir is right beside an immense out-of-town shopping centre, at a point where the River Don is surrounded and criss-crossed by rail routes and roads, including the M1. The first fig I spot is growing near a large Wetherspoon's pub. The tree is stout and bowl-shaped, with perky horizontal boughs that curve out, then up. It has multiple stems and its pale-grey bark is covered all over with nobbles. It's healthy-looking, full of vigour and vim, growing right on the water's edge. Its lower branches skim the surface and are snagged with litter. This stretch of river was canalized long ago to maximize the extent of the site surrounding it and to minimize flooding. There are large, light-industrial units and warehouses on the other side of the water, but only a few decades ago the industry here was much heavier.

From 1900 until the early 1980s, this part of the River Don was home to some of the biggest steel, engineering and arms factories in Europe. Before that, the area had been largely rural, a place of small-scale, water-powered forges and mills. It became increasingly industrial and polluted, and by the mid-1800s fish had disappeared from much of the river system. At the turn of the century, Robert Hadfield chose this site for a new steel plant. It expanded rapidly as a consequence of the arms race leading up to the First World War, and kept on growing. In 1914 he was employing 6,000 people, and by the end of the war 15,000. Hadfield became Sheffield's largest employer, and one of the world's leading metallurgists.

After the steelworks shut for good in the 1980s, the area was left derelict for nearly a decade, before work began on the Meadowhall shopping centre. Eventually this meant the River Don's banks were opened up to walkers and cyclists, and a riverside park was built. With heavy industry and its terrible pollution gone, the water quality began to improve, and now, at certain times of day, people see kingfishers, herons, grey wagtails, rabbits and bats here. Fish-eating birds are a sign of a healthy river, and the once-sickly Don is now thought to support species including eel, salmon, barbel, chub and dace.

Walking further along the waterway, away from town, I see several more fig trees growing on the Don's banks. A campaign in the 1990s means this exotic fruit forest now has protected status. Oliver Gilbert's obituary in *The Independent* in May 2005 described him as 'an authority on the ecology of urban wildlife, helping Sheffield to become the best-studied urban jungle in Britain after London'. Thanks to Gilbert, the health of his city's waterside figs is a matter of public concern, just like Ruminalis' was, back in the day. The trees are also a remarkable living connection with the city's polluted, industrial past.

ANOTHER FLESHY FRUIT WORTH KNOWING

There are two types of mulberry found in the UK, black (*Morus nigra*) and white (*Morus alba*). Both produce long, raspberry-like fruits. Black mulberries ripen to dark purple, while white mulberries are paler. Pyramus and Thisbe's ill-fated tryst took place under a mulberry tree, and Ovid's story has it that the white fruit was stained red with their blood after they killed themselves with the same sword. Urban squirrels love these trees, and in late summer will get drunk on fallen, fermenting fruit.

The white mulberry is also the foodstuff of the silkworm. King James I planted lots of mulberries in the seventeenth century – both black and white – and encouraged others to do the same, in a bid to start a home-grown silk industry. In *The Rings of Saturn*, W. G. Sebald describes how the monarch always had a casket of royal silkworms with him whenever he took a journey through his kingdom. Sebald also explains that Norwich later became home to a thriving community of Huguenot weavers who were central to the manufacture of silk goods. Their factories were apparently booming in the 1750s, creating fabrics of 'an iridescent, quite indescribable beauty ... like the plumage of birds'.

The hazels

There are around fifteen different types of hazel, growing as shrubs and small trees, plus several hybrids and ornamental cultivars. They all have toothed leaves, are covered with catkins in winter and spring, and produce edible nuts that are surrounded by frilly, leaf-like bracts. The Celts believed that hazelnuts, also known as cobnuts and filberts, were a source of wisdom and inspiration, while the Grimm Brothers' tale 'The Hazel Branch' claims the trees offer protection from creeping and slithering things, including adders. Cobnuts are still cultivated in Kent, but most of the hazelnuts eaten in the UK are now imported.

COMMON HAZEL

Corylus avellana

The hazel tree is also known as 'nuttery' and the 'filbert shrub'. Shakespeare's *Romeo and Juliet* is believed to be the first printed example of hazel being used in reference to eye colour.

Shape is many-stemmed and shrubby. (Fig. 28)

Leaves are softly fuzzy and floppy, with toothed, raggedy edges. (Fig. 29)

Bark is a pale metallic bronzed brown, smooth, but with fine lines and bumps.

Flowers are drooping yellow catkins (male), tiny red tufts (female), both on the same tree.

Fruit ripens into clusters of hazelnuts in the autumn. (Fig. 30)

Found in the thickets, hedges and woods of peri-urban places, including around Leeds.

Fig. 28

Fig. 29

Fig. 30

Hazel is valued for its nuts and for its fast-growing, whip-like shoots. It's not really a tree of the city centre; you're more likely to find it in the peri-urban, woody places that surround a town. And it doesn't actually look that much like a tree at all, tending to be small and shrub-like, with multiple stems sprouting up from the same, indefinitely self-renewing stump.

I head to Yorkshire to learn more about hazel and how it can be used, because that's where I'll find the Leeds Coppice Workers. They're a co-operative of city people who lead country lives, commuting out rather than in, to do their day-jobs. I arrive in Leeds early and wander the streets for a couple of hours, looking for trees mainly, but also ogling the city's arcades of upmarket shops. I admire cherries, hornbeams and hawthorns, mosaics, vaulted glass roofs and Vivienne Westwood suits, before returning to the station to wait for Dave, who is busy on a tai-chi course until half-past two. He shows up exactly on time in a battered silver car that has feathers hanging from the rear-view mirror and red plastic flowers on the dashboard.

First, Dave drives us to Leeds Coppice Workers' wood yard, a small patch of land on the outskirts of town, lent to the co-operative by the city council. It's part of a sprawling municipal nursery where the plants for Leeds' parks, roundabouts, flowerbeds and school grounds are grown. It's a quiet time for the coppice workers and there's only a small amount of wood left at the yard to be sold, but enough for Dave to demonstrate some of what he does. He shows me his favourite tool, the billhook, which has a wide, foldout blade that's about twenty centimetres long and curves at the tip. He uses it to slice through one of the slimmer hazel stems in seconds, with a series of precisely placed slashes. A crop of poles like this can be woven into fencing, he says, while thicker rods make good bean-poles, fence-posts and stakes. Trunks are cut into logs for firewood.

We get back in the car and drive north. Leeds is a city surrounded by countryside, with ridges of green that cut right into it, and main roads running in and out like spokes on a wheel. Even in the centre of town, now and then you'll glimpse fields in the distance. We drive through leafy, lime-lined streets and past Roundhay Park, which, at 700 acres, is one of the largest parks in Europe. The landscape quickly becomes rural, despite the fact that we're still only a few miles from the city centre.

Dave parks the car in a lay-by. The sky is beginning to bruise overhead. He pulls a golf umbrella out of the boot in anticipation, and I put on my waterproof jacket. We pass through a swing gate and into Hetchell Wood, a nature reserve run by Yorkshire Wildlife Trust. I soon realize the umbrella won't only offer shelter from the coming storm, but is also an effective tool for bashing brambles back. This is a small woodland, but one full of grand old beeches, some grown massive, including one that stands atop a steep siding where the soil must slip in heavy weather. This tree's characteristically shallow roots are exposed, and the network of woody branches below forms an earthy reflection of the beech's wide, spreading canopy above. There's a large silver birch here too, with white skin cracked into rough diamond shapes, and a still-standing but blackened oak that must have been struck by lightning.

::::

Coppicing is when a traditional woodworker cuts – or 'coppices' – tree stems back to their stump, waits for a new crop to grow, harvests them, waits again, harvests again, and so on in regular cycles, moving through a woodland, coppicing one discrete section – or 'coop' – at a time. The tree's ability to grow back in this way is one of the reasons we might hold our mega-flora in high esteem. Not only can trees outlive us by generations and provide us with fuel, food and fibre during that time, but they can also regenerate. In an interview for *The New Yorker*, plant physiologist Stefano Mancuso discusses why we should appreciate plants more, explaining, 'A plant has a modular design, so it can lose up to ninety per cent of its body without being killed ... There's nothing like that in the animal world. It creates a resilience.' It's a design and a resilience that we humans have taken advantage of.

Coppicing was well established in England by the early 1080s, and was practised in almost all woods by 1251. As a result, woodlands can be places as much shaped by human hands as towns and cities are, albeit in different ways. The hazels in Hetchell Wood, like many other trees in many other coppice woods, could be called culturally modified, cajoled by human hands to deliver a steady crop of wood. The character of both the trees and the woodland where they grow has been altered as a result. It's not just us who benefits from this. Yorkshire Wildlife Trust invited coppice workers into the wood because the practice lets the light in and so encourages germination, new growth and more wildlife. As Sara Maitland says in *Gossip from the Forest*, the relationship between a wood and its people has the potential to be symbiotic rather than exploitative, and woodland can flourish under good human management. Rather than seeing the forest as something dangerous that has to be tamed, it can be 'an infinite resource', rich and generous.

Leeds Coppice Workers have a few coops in Hetchell Wood, all at different stages. The first one Dave takes me to has been fenced off for a few years now, to stop deer, dogs and people accessing it, and the hazel regrowing inside is tall and thick. The second coop we visit was cut only a few months ago. It's also closed off, but it's still possible to see exactly where the chainsaws and billhooks have been. This coop is steep, with a rocky limestone outcrop, and must have been hard to work. As part of the coppicing process, great piles of clippings, or 'brash', have been left behind – rather than being a waste product, they are used to provide cover for wildlife, before rotting down and enriching the soil. Importantly, from the perspective of a coppice worker, the brash also protects new growth from browsing rabbits and squirrels that fences can't keep out. The hazel here is springing back vigorously and some stems are already half a metre high.

Coppicing is done in coops like this so that there are always areas of cover alongside those that have been opened up. Leeds Coppice Workers only coppice in the autumn and winter, and stop by the end of February when the birds start to nest. They never coppice a coop adjacent to one that has recently been cut. As it starts to rain steadily, I wonder whether this is a tough way to make a living, not least when the weather's like this. Dave explains that there's good appetite locally for the woodland products that all their work creates and, as well as the usual posts, poles, charcoal and firewood, the co-operative gets some more curious requests. Recent ones include tree trunks for a theatre production, and freshly cut logs for cultivating edible mushrooms on – the grower impregnates the log with mushroom spawn, then cares for it almost as if it were a shade-loving plant, waiting patiently for the spawn to fruit. Coppice work is seasonal, and membership of the co-operative expands and contracts. The money is okay, but all of them have to supplement their coppice work with other jobs. But Dave insists he likes the variety and flexibility of part-time self-employment, and he enjoys being outside, especially when the weather is good. Not now then, I think, noticing how the wet is starting to seep through my unsuitable shoes and into my socks. It's time to leave. I follow Dave, unsure of quite where we've been or how to get out.

Walking through Hetchell Wood is markedly different from my earlier wander through Leeds, in terms of sights, smells and sounds, but in some ways it's the same. Encountering the city for the first time, and without a plan or looking at a map, I walked aimlessly and soon lost track of exactly where I was. Leeds gave me an anonymous warren of streets and buildings to disappear into, and no long views from which to orientate myself. In

The Tree, John Fowles remarks that 'Older and less planned quarters of cities and towns can be profoundly woodlike ... the way they unreel, disorientate, open, close, surprise, please.' As I trail behind Dave, trying not to become preoccupied with my sodden feet, and instead mulling over everything he's told me about coppicing and his unusually rural urban life, I start to think that cities and woods are indeed rather alike. Both are places to get lost, find yourself again and emerge with something new.

ANOTHER HAZEL WORTH KNOWING

While Turkish hazel (*Corylus colurna*) has typically toothed leaves and characteristic catkins, it grows much larger than the common hazel. Its foliage is more polished, those catkins are more showy and its nuts are bigger, each one clothed in a fabulously shaggy coat. Rather than being shrubby and multi-stemmed, the Turkish hazel has a single straight trunk and a neat conical canopy. It has a formal look that has historically made it popular for civic planting schemes, while tree expert Owen Johnson suggests it has been grown in UK gardens from as early as 1582. It copes well with drought, heat, frost and flooding, which is why today you might see it planted along urban avenues and streets, and in car parks. In his field guide, *London's Street Trees*, Paul Wood points out that the rigours of urban street life are pretty similar to the stresses of the Turkish hazel's native mountainside habitat. In city settings, grey squirrels have become big fans of its large nuts.

The horse chestnuts

The small horse-chestnut family includes the American buckeyes, along with a few ornamental hybrids. These trees have large, palmate leaves and eye-catching clusters of flowers in spring, followed by polished, conker-like nuts in autumn. The genus has a strong connection with Ohio in the United States, which is known as the 'buckeye state', and where local people are affectionately called 'buckeyes'.

HORSE CHESTNUT

Aesculus hippocastanum

'*Aesculus*' means edible acorn, despite the fact that this tree's nuts are toxic. The first part of the tree's common name is most probably derived from its association with horse medicine, although 'horse' could also be used to imply the tree's large size. The second part acknowledges the fact that conkers look so similar to sweet chestnuts.

Shape is large, twisting and tall. (Fig. 31)

Leaves are compound, made up of five to seven large, toothed leaflets arranged in a circle. (Fig. 32)

Bark is grey at first, becoming reddish-brown and coarse with age.

Flowers are upright white spires, like dollops of whipped cream from a distance. (Fig. 33)

Fruit are polished brown conkers encased in spiky green jackets.

Found in parks and gardens, and planted in formal rows along urban avenues.

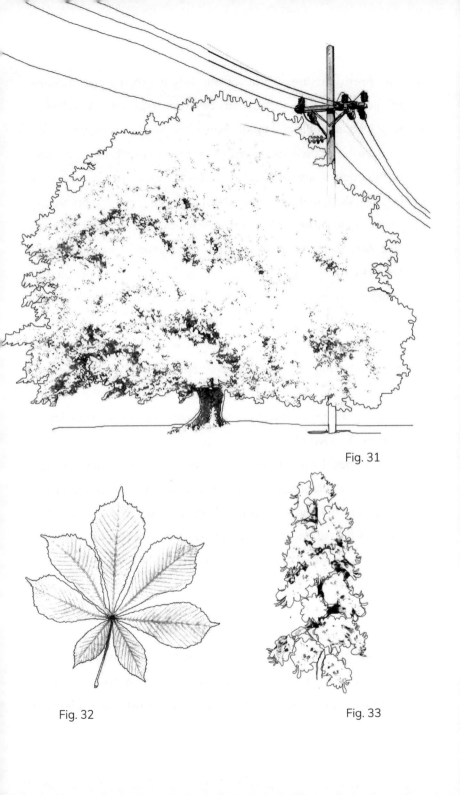

Fig. 31

Fig. 32

Fig. 33

The horse chestnut is one of our largest urban trees, and one of the most easily recognized, because of its nuts. Conkers – which are inedible and mildly poisonous, but are rumoured once to have been used medicinally to treat hoarse horses suffering from coughs – are unmistakable. A spiky green jacket conceals a beige-bellied, mahogany-brown nut, which is always appealingly smooth and glossy when first prised out of its protective coat. The first game of conkers – or 'conquerors' – is thought to have been played on the Isle of Wight in 1848, and people still compete to prove theirs is the toughest nut today, including at the annual World Conker Championships in Northamptonshire. Conkers are everywhere in autumn – hailing down from on high, cluttering up parks and pavements alike. There's something satisfying about the way trees litter bland city streets like this, first in spring with spent blossom, then in autumn with rotting leaves and smashed fruit.

Although I love conkers, and will always slip a silky nut into my pocket whenever I come across one, I actually enjoy the horse chestnut more in spring these days, when it's in new leaf and full flower. It's the perfect park tree to sit under, if you're craving a pool of deep shade. The large leaves are palmate, or hand-like, with five to seven fat fingers radiating out in a circle from a central point. They're bright green when they first emerge, floppy and tender, becoming darker and tougher with age. But it's the blossom that really makes this tree distinct. The nectar-rich flowers are clustered into upright spires that can be thirty centimetres long. Up close, you'll see that each off-white bloom is splashed inside with hot pink. From afar, the flower spikes look like generous dollops of whipped cream, making the horse chestnut the kind of tree you might find growing in the edible garden of Willy Wonka's chocolate factory.

⸭

Brought over from Turkey in the late 1500s, the horse chestnut has since been planted widely in urban and suburban areas across Europe. Along with lime and plane, it has proved a popular choice for grand boulevards, particularly in Paris. Numerous ordinary residential streets in the UK are named after the chestnut, while one of our most majestic Chestnut Avenues is in Bushy Park, west London. A mile long, it was designed by Christopher Wren and was planted in 1699 as a formal approach to William III and Mary II's palace at Hampton Court. The Victorian tradition of celebrating Chestnut Sunday along its length every May continues to this day – it's one of the only days when the avenue is closed to cars.

Visiting on the Friday before Chestnut Sunday, my first glimpse of the avenue comes from the Teddington end of the park. It's a straight road, bordered by a clipped lawn and a single row of horse chestnuts set back on each side. There must be many hundreds of trees here. Viewed as a sweep, their lush canopies look conjoined into two thick parallel lines. The overall effect is regimented, well dressed rather than beautiful. It makes me think of military parades, where masses of people stand to attention in strict formation, all in uniform. It's a spectacle of trees, designed to impress and intimidate. Only someone as rich and powerful as royalty could afford to plant and maintain such an avenue. The beauty of it is that – just like a human crowd, which on the surface seems anonymous – up close each member of the group is an individual. Some of the chestnuts are stout and spreading, others are tall and slim; some are massive, others small; some young, others old. Their flowers and leaves may all be alike, but the way their boughs and branches crack and twist is not.

Feeling hungry and contemplative, I sit down to eat an overpriced cheese-and-tomato toastie under one of the trees. I face away from the road and into the park, with my back pressed up against the chestnut's rough trunk, which is crusted all over with bright-yellow lichen. Its leaves have something of a parasol shape, combining to cast a solid shadow that couldn't be called dappled. It's an unusually hot day for May and the shelter is welcome. All I can see is green, but all I can hear is traffic. Preparations are under way for Sunday's festivities – marquees are being erected, Portaloos installed, temporary fencing staked out, fairground rides set up. A curious young crow takes an interest in me, or perhaps my sandwich, keeping its distance, but definitely checking me out. I stare back. Its feathers look midnight-blue in the midday sun.

The crow eventually loses interest and hops away, and I pull Jean-Paul Sartre's *Nausea* out of my bag, which I've purposely brought with me to read in the presence of the horse chestnuts. For Sartre's protagonist, Antoine Roquentin – his eyes glued to the root of a park chestnut as it plunges into the earth –

this tree can reveal everything about what it means to be in the world. As he stares at the 'black, knotty mass', Roquentin suddenly understands what it means to exist, after enduring days of excruciating uneasiness. Existence is not a harmless 'abstract category', rather it is 'the very stuff of things', and the chestnut root, though inert, is steeped in it. Roquentin's epiphany is that 'the diversity of things, their individuality, was only an appearance, a veneer' – and behind that veneer, the root, the tree, himself and everyone around him were 'soft, monstrous masses, in disorder ...'

Sartre has some great descriptions of the chestnut tree – its black and blistered bark is like 'boiled leather' and is covered halfway up in 'green rust'. The root itself is 'a big, rugged paw' with 'sea-lion skin' and an 'oily, horny, stubborn look'. The park fills Roquentin's nose with a 'green, putrid smell'. He decides that 'If you existed, you had to *exist to that extent*, to the point of mildew, blisters, obscenity.' As Roquentin, a writer and an historian, loses his grip on language, he realizes that the root, the tree, is 'beneath all explanation'. The wordsmith finds there are simply no words. When he finally gets up to leave, the municipal park and the chestnut tree smile back at him conspiratorially.

::::

Avenue planting is visually striking, but monocultures of all kinds are a risk. When the same species grows in dense, uniform rows like those on Bushy Park's Chestnut Avenue, each tree is left more vulnerable to attack. If one tree gets blight, they're all likely to catch it. Horse chestnuts across Europe are suffering at the moment from three diseases: the leaf-mining moth, leaf-blotch fungus and bleeding canker. None of these kill the tree, but they do leave it looking shabby. The leaf-miner is having a particularly noticeable impact in the UK, turning leaves a sorry shade of brown in the height of summer and affecting conker crops.

Trees are long-lived but they don't live for ever – if disease doesn't get them, then harsh weather might, or a combination of the two. One of the world's most famous urban horse chestnuts crashed down in 2010, but its memory lives on in hundreds of saplings grown from its conkers. Known as the 'Anne Frank Tree', it was 170 years old when it died, and grew in the courtyard garden of 188 Keizersgracht, the house where the teenage diarist hid. It was visible from an attic window throughout the Frank family's stay there during the Second World War, and Anne wrote about it three times, in February, April and May 1944.

Anne's feelings about the horse chestnut become entwined with her feelings about Peter, an older boy who is also hiding in the attic. On 23 February 1944 she writes, '[Peter and I] looked out at the blue sky, the bare chestnut tree glistening with dew, the seagulls and other birds glinting with silver as they swooped through the air, and we were so moved and entranced that we couldn't speak.' The chestnut blossoms as their love does. By 13 May, the tree is in full flower and 'even more beautiful than last year'.

Anne becomes increasingly preoccupied with nature during what turn out to be her final weeks in the attic. In early May of

1944 she writes, 'Everyday I feel myself maturing, I feel liberation approaching, I feel the beauty of nature and the goodness of the people around me.' Later that month she wonders whether it might have been better if they hadn't gone into hiding and if they were all dead now. 'But we all shrink from this thought. We still love life, we haven't yet forgotten the voice of nature, and we keep hoping, hoping for ... everything.' By mid-June, Anne admits that she has become quite 'mad about nature' and it's likely that her confinement is the cause. She's explicit about the solace it offers her, writing that 'looking at the sky, the clouds, the moon and stars really does make me feel calm and hopeful. It's much better medicine than valerian or bromide. Nature makes me feel humble and ready to face every blow with courage!'

Anne's fate makes what she writes heartbreaking, but there's so much hope here too. Her connection with the horse-chestnut tree, and with nature more widely, proves how important these natural anchors can be, even in the very worst of times. Where Antoine Roquentin's chestnut tree becomes the lurid manifestation of his existential crisis, Anne Frank finds hers to be something solid to hold on to while the world around her falls apart.

ANOTHER CHESTNUT WORTH KNOWING

Thought to have been introduced to the UK by the Romans, who used its nuts to make flour, the sweet chestnut (*Castanea sativa*) isn't actually related to the horse chestnut, but the two trees share a common name because their nuts look so alike. Sweet chestnuts – the ones we traditionally eat roasted in winter, especially at Christmas – are large, glossy and brown and grow inside spiky green jackets, just like conkers. But, other than their nuts, and the fact that both can grow to be large and impressive, the trees' different foliage and flowers make them easy to tell apart. Where the horse chestnut's leaves are palmate, the sweet chestnut's are narrow and long, growing up to twenty-five centimetres, with sharply serrated edges. The sweet chestnut has long, yellowish flowers that look like fluffy pipe-cleaners, and which dendrologist Owen Johnson thinks smell of fried mushrooms. Planted as a street tree as well as in gardens and parks, the sweet chestnut can live for 700 years.

The limes

There are several different types of lime tree, all with heart-shaped leaves. Their small, intoxicating flowers burst open on the end of long stalks, and their fruits are tiny and round. Lime trees were once associated with fertility, and were used as a symbol of liberty in Switzerland and France. They are not to be confused with the citrus fruit.

COMMON LIME

Tilia × europaea

'Lime' stems from various words meaning flexible, lithe or yielding, including the Old English '*lind*'.

Shape is tall and impressive, with leaves and whiskery branches growing low down on the trunk. (Fig. 34)

Leaves are bright green, lopsided hearts with serrated edges; shiny and sticky to touch. (Fig. 35)

Bark is pale greyish-brown, vertically ridged and bossed.

Flowers are sweet-smelling starbursts, tiny and yellow, dangling on the end of long stalks. (Fig. 36)

Fruit are small, round, green and downy, also on long stalks, with a wing at the top.

Found in cities across Europe, planted in formal rows along urban avenues.

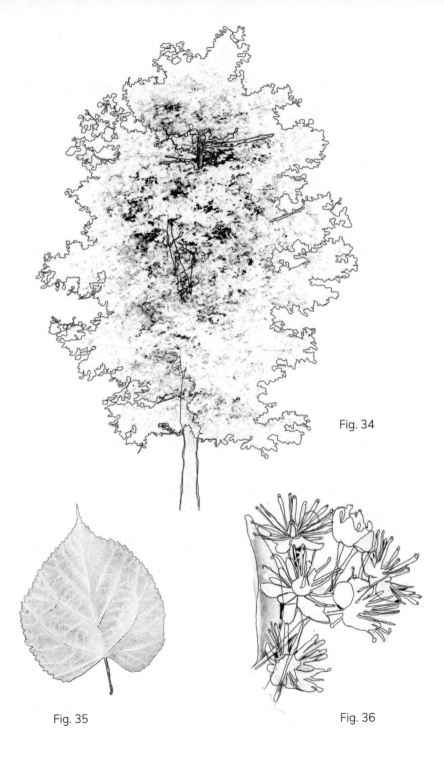

Fig. 34

Fig. 35

Fig. 36

The common lime was a happy accident. It's a hybrid between small-leaved lime and broad-leaved lime, a merger that is believed to have occurred in the wild, rather than in the greenhouse. That said, many of the common limes you'll meet will have been planted. The species became fashionable from the seventeenth century on, valued by plantsmen and women because it is fast-growing and easily propagated from suckers. Today the lime is one of our most magnificent urban trees, a species that truly makes a city leafy. It's tall and long-lived, with the potential to reach forty metres high and 500 years old. Like the horse chestnut and London plane, it's frequently seen pollarded into a uniform shape along formal avenues and boulevards – a street tree that softens cities' hard edges. Also known as 'linden', lime is widely planted across Europe as well as the UK. One of Berlin's most well-known streets, Unter den Linden, takes its name from the lime tree. Running from the City Palace to the Brandenburg Gate, the boulevard's original trees were planted in 1647. Today it's not nearly so leafy, but a few lindens do still grow along its length.

Lime foliage sprouts low down on the trunk as well as high up. The leaves are roughly heart-shaped with finely toothed edges, although the heart is always lopsided, with one side slightly bigger than the other. In summer, the leaves look as if they've been sloppily varnished, covered in a sticky honeydew that is produced by a lime-loving aphid, which in turn is loved by aphid-eaters, such as ladybirds, hoverflies and moths. The honeydew can sometimes drip right off the tree – gluey deposits on your car bonnet can be a sign that you've parked under a lime. The tree has distinctive blossom too, which tends to bloom when the days are long and hot. Lime flowers are tiny yellow starbursts on the end of long green stems, which hang from the tree in loose clusters. They're fragrant and adored by insects. The honey produced by bees that have feasted on lime flowers is said to be some of the finest-tasting, which is one of the reasons why urban honey is so good to eat.

Lime blossom isn't just for the bees. The flowers can be harvested, dried and used to make a calming herbal tea. In his *Tree Medicine* guide, herbalist Peter Conway recommends it as an infusion that will ease 'irritable states, aid sleep, soothe coughs and clear colds'. It has a delicate honeyed aroma that for Marcel Proust can fuel time-travel. In *Remembrance of Things Past* there is a long passage where our narrator recalls helping his great-aunt prepare a restorative lime-blossom tisane, into which she then dips a little madeleine for him to eat. Emptying a package carefully prepared by his aunt's chemist, our narrator finds the drying lime-stems twisted into 'a fantastic trellis' of the 'most decorative poses'. Falling into a daydream as the tea brews, he imagines the 'moony, tender glow which lit up the blossoms among the frail forest of stems from which they hung like little golden roses'. The rest of the lime's foliage has changed beyond all recognition, now more like the 'transparent wings of flies or the blank sides of labels'. Once the infusing is complete, our narrator savours the way his aunt is soothed by the dead-blossom tea.

⁙

Linden trees have inspired other artists too. Beethoven is famous for having had a close relationship with a lime tree just outside Vienna, which he's said to have hugged daily in the summer of 1803 when composing his third symphony. In 'Ludwig Van Beethoven's Return to Vienna', the poet Rita Dove describes the courtyard that the composer saw when he looked out of his window: there a 'linden tree twined skyward, leafy umbilicus canted toward light, warped in the very act of yearning'. Although the symphony was originally dedicated to Napoleon Bonaparte, Beethoven withdrew the honour, renaming the final piece 'Eroica', or the 'Heroic Symphony', after the French military leader declared himself emperor and betrayed the ideals of the French Revolution.

I go and hear a performance of the 'Eroica' at Milton Court in London. As I listen, I imagine Beethoven gripping his tree, chest pressed tightly to it, arms a hoop, thinking of Napoleon's exploits while the music roars through him. The lime's leaves would surely have shaken with the force of it. The symphony is performed by the Guildhall Chamber Orchestra, and the young musicians' exhilaration is obvious. I start wondering what the piece is like to perform, rather than just listen to. My friend Ria, who is a violinist, says that performing anything by Beethoven requires superhuman levels of concentration, because his music is so emotionally demanding. She explains that it's important to play Beethoven sensitively, always listening to everyone else in the orchestra, to ensure that you sing out or step back at the right times.

I ask Ria about all this just after she's attended Israeli violinist

Maxim Vengerov's latest masterclass at the Royal College of Music. She's written down something he said: 'The drama in Beethoven is everything. Behind every note – the harmony, the modulation – there's a story. There must be a different interpretation every time you play it. Tell the story: it's your story. Only you can feel the drama.' For me, on the night I hear the 'Eroica' performed live, I find myself thinking mainly about the act of composition, and the forces that fed into it. I think of the lime tree as much as the emperor, and I think of John Berger, who said in his essay 'The White Bird' that 'Art is an organised response to what nature allows us to glimpse occasionally.' A powerful piece of music has the potential to transport you wherever you want to go, to tell you a new story each time you come to it. A tree as captivating as Beethoven's linden can do the same.

My favourite storyteller about the lime is Etel Adnan. In her poetry she conjures up 'gardens where, linden trees get ready for, a lunar voyage', which makes me think of their energetic sprays of starburst flowers, and their tall, majestic forms, striving upwards. In 'Linden Trees', the picture Adnan paints is more startling – a lime's tender leaves trembling like a 'battered girl' and its branches 'snorting like a horse'. Although I associate this syrupy tree with summer weather that's hot and still, this is how the lime looks and sounds when the weather is rough and ruinous. Or when a composer has wrapped his arms around it, electrifying music flowing right through him and it.

ANOTHER LIME WORTH KNOWING

The ornamental silver lime (*Tilia tomentosa*) has a domed shape and toothy, heart-shaped leaves that, unlike common lime's, are pale and woolly underneath. This tree can flip its foliage in hot weather so that the white undersides reflect the sun, making it a good choice as our cities get hotter and drier. Its sugary nectar is soapy and strong; in fact it's so powerful that it can incapacitate some insects. One of Romania's most famous poets, Mihai Eminescu, is believed to have written some of his best work while sitting under a silver lime in the city of Iaşi. The tree is still standing and, at around 500 years old, it has been called by *Lonely Planet* one of Romania's most important natural monuments.

The maidenhairs

The maidenhair tree found in UK cities today is the sole surviving member of a family that thrived between sixty-five and 250 million years ago, during the Mesozoic Era. Also known as the age of reptiles, this era includes the Triassic, Jurassic and Cretaceous periods. During this time dinosaurs roamed the land, as it gradually split up from one large continent into several smaller ones. Other Mesozoic plants included ferns, horsetails and conifers.

MAIDENHAIR TREE
Ginkgo biloba

'*Ginkgo*' comes from the Chinese '*yin-hing*', meaning silver apricot and describing the female tree's fruits, while '*biloba*' refers to the fact that both male and female trees' leaves are split into two lobes – they're bi-lobed.

Shape is tall and slender, but also dishevelled and shaggy. (Fig. 37)

Leaves are fan- or butterfly-shaped, turning yellow in autumn. (Fig. 38)

Bark is grey-brown and corky, becoming ridged and barnacled.

Flowers are yellow catkins (male), green nobbles (female), on separate trees.

Fruit is fleshy and foul-smelling. (Fig. 39)

Found along city streets, and in parks and botanic gardens.

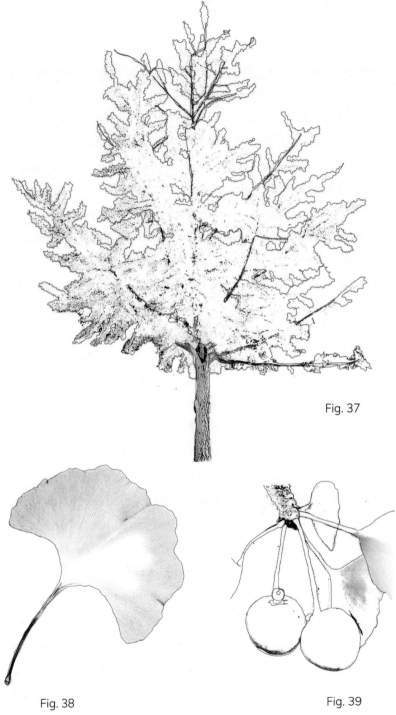

Fig. 37

Fig. 38

Fig. 39

The maidenhair tree is easy to spot because its leaves have a shape unlike any others you'll find in the urban forest. Like the half-unfolded wings of a butterfly, with the outline of an outspread fan, they're similar to those of the maidenhair fern, but, because few of us know our ferns, and Ginkgo biloba extract is a familiar health supplement, this is a tree commonly known by its botanical name. A fresh, fluttery matt-green throughout spring and summer, ginkgo foliage becomes butter-coloured in autumn, before pouring all over the pavement. The tree has a shape that is both elegant and dishevelled. Its slender, upright profile is mussed up by branches that stick out at all angles, while its greyish bark becomes wizened and warty with age.

Unlike the rest of the trees that grow in the sylvan city, the maidenhair has no living relatives anywhere else in the world. It's the only remaining member of the Ginkgoaceae family, which was successful in the Mesozoic Era. These trees saw mountain ranges form and the dinosaurs come and go. Tree-pollen deposits in the soil suggest there were maidenhair trees in Britain millions of years ago, although the ginkgo eventually died out. It's thought to have arrived back here in 1760, imported from China as an ornamental exotic. This tree is 'dioecious', which means that it's either male or female, but never both. Males are usually grown in the UK, as females produce a foul-smelling fruit known as the 'silver apricot', which causes a slimy mess when it drops and rots. The first ginkgo I ever met was male and massive, growing in the tiny front garden of a terraced house in north-east London. The golden leaf litter around it was so strangely shaped that I felt compelled to find out what it was. Since then I've noticed more and more young maidenhairs being planted around town, including an entire row outside the building where I work. Once mostly found in botanic gardens, where they would be some of the more noteworthy and prized specimens, you're now increasingly likely to see ginkgos growing along city streets, selected by urban tree officers for their capacity to survive pretty much anything the world cares to throw at them. In polluted cities facing up to the realities of a changing climate and the extreme weather conditions that is bringing, the ginkgo seems to be a tree that we can rely on to cope. It's a fair assumption, because it has good form as a survivor, having already made it through mass extinctions and entire epochs.

Today the ginkgo attracts awe among tree-lovers because of what happened in Hiroshima. When the atomic bomb flattened the Japanese city on 6 August 1945, very little survived, but somehow a few of its blasted ginkgo trees sent out new shoots. From deep within the cancerous soil, their resilient roots were refusing to wither. Here was something small to cling onto during a moment of darkest despair. Or at least it has become something to cling onto since, with the survivors grown into large trees that people make a point of visiting. Hiroshima's ginkgos offer a welcome diversion from horror towards hope.

In the same way that the flowering cherry has become the archetypal tree of peace, the ginkgo is seen as the ultimate survivor tree, although other species attain this status too. When a catastrophe befalls a city, trees can become mainstays from which to remember, rebuild and recover. In New York a handful of trees that grew in the vicinity of the World Trade Center managed to stay standing after the attacks on 11 September 2001. The Living Memorial Grove beside Brooklyn Bridge contains callery pears and lime trees that were rescued from Ground Zero and transplanted. Saplings grown from pear seeds have also been planted in other parts of the city. In 'Co-creators of Memory, Metaphors for Resilience, and Mechanisms for Recovery', a paper about living memorials, Heather McMillen, Lindsay Campbell and Erika Svendsen explain how important trees have been to some New Yorkers since 9/11. The women's research has uncovered that, in a post-disaster landscape, some people find planting and tending trees to be a way to do something positive at a time when they otherwise feel helpless. They conclude, 'Through the collaborative work of planting and caring for flora in memorials, grief became embodied and processed.'

Survivor trees have the potential to become powerful symbols of renewal then, but they can also highlight our failures and flaws, and our temporariness. Individual ginkgos can live for hundreds of years, while the species is sure to outlive the human race. Its family has been around for millennia, while we've been here for just the blink of an eye. With one foot in the deep past and the other in the far future, the ginkgo tree reminds us of our vulnerability and insignificance, and it will surely be what any dystopian future is foliated with.

In *The Drowned World*, J. G. Ballard describes a silted-up city dissolving beneath a searing, white-hot sun. Only the very tops of high-rises are left visible, the rest being submerged within lagoons that are populated by giant basilisks and iguanas, and fringed by dense groves. Trees have leaves like huge sails and form forests with canopies 200 feet high. I imagine them as ginkgos, future-proof street trees grown gigantic with all that sun and fertile silt, their fan-shaped leaves now outrageously oversized. Our hero, Kerans, is one of the only people left in this landscape. He navigates mainly by boat and is in fear mostly of the sun. He sometimes muses on the fact that 'the genealogical tree of mankind was systematically pruning itself', moving backwards towards a point when a second Adam and Eve might find themselves alone in a new Eden. Ballard's book speaks to contemporary fears about rising sea levels and flooded-out cities, of a climate too hot for human life – visions that are already becoming a reality in some parts of the world.

While Ballard's drowned world feels like a warning, there's something breathtaking about it too. Nature reclaiming the city is a popular trope, one that is as romantic as it is terrifying. In *The Wind in the Willows*, the wild wood grows on the site of an old city, one that the rich and powerful people who lived there thought would last for ever. As Badger explains, 'It was all down, down, down gradually – ruin and levelling and disappearance. Then it was all up, up, up, gradually, as seeds grew to saplings, and saplings to forest trees, and bramble and fern came creeping in to help.' Trees, including the ancient ginkgo, can be part of landscapes that are both catastrophic and sublime.

ANOTHER BULLETPROOF TREE WORTH KNOWING

The fast-growing Caucasian wingnut (*Pterocarya fraxinifolia*) – also known as the Caucasian walnut – has compound leaves, with elliptical leaflets arranged along a central stalk. It grows to be wide and tall, often with multiple stems and suckers around its base. With foliage similar to an ash – hence the *fraxinifolia* part of its botanical name – what makes the wingnut stand out are its jolly tassels of winged nuts, which can be half a metre long. Native to the Caucasus and Alborz mountains, this wingnut was introduced to the UK sometime after 1800. Tree expert Owen Johnson says it has 'vandal-proof vigour', making it an increasingly popular choice for town parks.

The maples

There are well over 100 different types of maple, with leaves that typically have five lobes and are displayed in opposite pairs along the branch. Most are deciduous, but there are some evergreens. They range in size from small and shrub-like to forty-five metres tall and are renowned for their autumn colour. Some maples are tapped for their syrup, while all maples produce bunches of double-winged fruits, which the poet John Clare described as being the shape of a stag's horn. With help from the wind, these spin off the tree in autumn, helicoptering away to colonize new ground.

SYCAMORE

Acer pseudoplatanus

'*Pseudoplatanus*' means like a plane tree or false plane, while 'sycamore' is a biblical word for a shade-giving tree that has been used in the UK to describe maples since the 1580s.

Shape is large, upright and domed, like a giant broccoli floret. (Fig. 40)

Leaves are dark green and glazed, each with five lobes and a serrated edge. (Fig. 41)

Bark is pinkish-brown-grey, becoming cracked and scaly with age.

Flowers are small and yellow-green, loosely clustered into drooping tassels.

Fruit are seeds encased in a flat wing, twinned and bunched, ripening red and brown. (Fig. 42)

Found in urban parks, gardens and railway sidings.

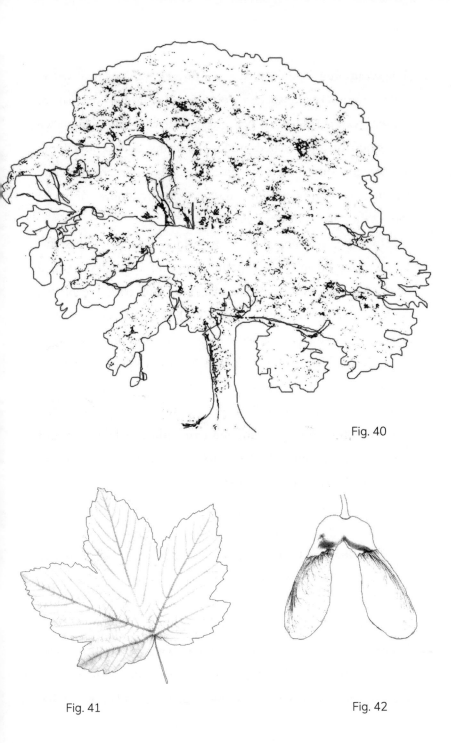

Fig. 40

Fig. 41

Fig. 42

The sycamore is a resilient tree that thrives in urban areas where other, more sensitive species would not. Living for 400 years or more, it can reach a great size and height, with a domed crown supported by upstretched arms. The trunk and central limbs are straight, surrounded by smaller branches that are tight and twisting. In summer, from a distance, the sycamore silhouette looks rather like a broccoli floret.

Up close, sycamore leaves are palmate. Each leaf has five lobes, and each lobe has a pointed tip and a roughly toothed edge. The foliage is similar to that of a plane tree, except that sycamore leaves are often glazed. This honeydew is excreted by aphids, which tempt in aphid-eating insects and, in turn, attract insect-eating birds and bats. Species like ladybirds, swallows and house martins rely on the sycamore for protein, while bees love its nectar-rich tassels of yellow flowers. Sticky foliage and sugar-sweet blooms are why author and tree enthusiast Fiona Stafford describes the sycamore as 'an apian and avian cafeteria' in her book *The Long, Long Life of Trees*.

::::

I became attached to the urban sycamore while living intimately with one in Holloway. Now subsumed into the inner city, this area was once the main cattle-driving route into London from the north. Back then, it would have been wooded and rural. A holloway is a sunken path, one 'worn down by the traffic of ages and the fretting of water', tree-lined and made tunnel-like where those trees' canopies curve to meet in the middle, as Stanley

Donwood so gloriously illustrates for Robert Macfarlane and Dan Richards' book of the same name. The Holloway sycamore grew in our downstairs neighbours' back garden, and its broad limbs hugged our tiny first-floor flat. As I stared out of my bedroom window and deep into its canopy daily, it became obvious how much local wildlife relied on this tree. On a summer's night it seethed with insects, and in the small hours the birds it hosted performed a dawn chorus that was loud enough to drown out the night-buses thundering up the Camden Road.

I became obsessed with this sycamore. Some days I would see a great spotted woodpecker skirting busily up, down and around its trunk, while at dusk it would occasionally be circled by a tiny pipistrelle bat. My bedroom had a second door in it that opened onto a flat section of roof, where I started making a garden in the sycamore's shade. It was out there that I learned the tree had its own weather. Not only did it make the invisible wind manifest, and sometimes shake out its damp the way dogs do, soaking me if I happened to be on the roof, but it also had a climate all its own – it might be steamy and humid beneath it one day, cool but dry the next.

I knew the Holloway tree was a sycamore because of its twinned, winged fruits, which became obvious as summer shifted into autumn. The botanical name for these is 'samaras', meaning winged nuts, but I've always called them 'whirligigs'. The fruits would start off green, before blushing red and brown. When the wind caught them, they would spiral off the tree with a helicopter motion, pitching off in pairs to conquer new ground.

These whirligigs are unmistakable: any tree that has them is sure to be a maple of some kind.

Leonardo da Vinci came up with the first design for a human-powered helicopter in 1493 – centuries before an actual helicopter took flight – after studying the way samaras spin off maple trees. He probably hypothesized that, if something can spiral down in the controlled way a whirligig does, surely something could also be engineered to spiral up. Da Vinci regularly took inspiration from the natural world in this way, also designing a flying machine based on a bat's wing and an armoured tank based on a turtle's shell. He wrote in one of his notebooks that human subtlety 'will never devise an invention more beautiful, more simple or more direct than does Nature, because in her inventions nothing is lacking, and nothing is superfluous'.

⁙

The sycamore was introduced to Britain in the sixteenth century, becoming naturalized in the eighteenth. A vigorous and efficient self-seeder and sender out of suckers, it's found in towns and cities across the UK today, and is the most common tree in both Edinburgh and London. As well as growing where it has been purposely planted, it also grows where it has planted itself. It likes to colonize commuter routes, whether or not that infrastructure is still in use. In autumn, sycamore is one of the species guilty of causing delays due to 'leaves on the line'. Network Rail, which manages the UK's rail infrastructure, uses this as an excuse for deeply unpopular mass-fellings. In 2018, a leaked internal document revealed an £800-million, five-year scheme to remove 'all leaf fall species' – so all deciduous trees – from within falling distance of Network Rail-run tracks. Sycamore was a key target, along with poplar, chestnut, lime and ash. *The Guardian* reported that 30,000 trees had already been cut down on the west-coast mainline between London and Carlisle in the twelve months to February 2017, with no plans to plant replacements. People living close to railway lines were unsurprisingly horrified – large trees screen their homes from the unwelcome sights, sounds and pollution of speeding trains.

It's perhaps easy for someone who travels mostly by bike to say, but a few delays caused by leaves on the line seem tolerable to me in exchange for everything else the sycamore and its fellow trackside trees offer. And just as the sycamore is a crucial tree for wildlife, so rail routes can be valuable habitats. If their sidings are left to run a little wild, they can provide cover for creatures to shelter in, and unbroken green corridors for them to move safely across town.

When rail infrastructure falls out of use altogether, it can be fully reclaimed by nature. There are abandoned train lines in cities that have been reinvented into leafy woodland walks, with abundant sycamore becoming an important part of the flora. Around Edinburgh, the Water of Leith flows from the Pentland Hills to the Firth of Forth. Once lined with mills, almost thirteen miles of the route have now been given over to cyclists and walkers, with the six miles between Balerno and Slateford following the course of an old railway line. It's a bit of a wormhole, one that allows you to wend your way through Edinburgh while feeling you're in the middle of nowhere. Being low down and enveloped over, the surrounding city is seen only in snatches, and always framed by trees. Meanwhile in north London, the two-and-a-half-mile Parkland Walk follows the route of a railway line that once connected Alexandra Palace with Finsbury Park, passing through Crouch End and Highgate. Passenger services stopped on the line in 1954, it closed completely in the early 1970s and then reopened as the Parkland Walk in 1984. In the decades since the rails were removed, hundreds of trees have grown up along the embankments. Sycamore, oak, ash, hawthorn and cherry arrived of their own volition or were already there; fig escaped from someone's back garden; while black poplar and hazel have been introduced. It's a short but magical walk, hidden away and with a secret air. It has the look and feel of a holloway in fact.

These wooded, car-free routes through capital cities are rightly loved by local people, and they prove the author Jonathan Raban right. In 'Second Nature', an essay written for *Granta*, he argues that we have 'a genius for incorporating industrial and technological change into [our] versions of both nature and the picturesque'. Places like the Water of Leith and the Parkland Walk are great examples of abandoned infrastructure and industrial lands re-formed and reclaimed to become urban woods, of which the sycamore is a vital member.

I still think of that large sycamore that branched out over my now long-lost roof-garden in Holloway, of its daytime woodpecker and its night-time bat. I'm certain it was that tree and that garden that made me fall in love with urban nature. Right now, I'm in a new-ish relationship with a tiny maple, which grows in a plant pot and is entirely portable. This is important when you live on a boat. The tree and I have been together for about three years. She has delicate maroon leaves that look like a shoal of starfish, and I find her immeasurably beautiful. She reaches up to my armpits, and spreads her branches as wide as about two of me. I worry about how vulnerable she seems when she is naked in winter, and I'm astonished by her vigour every spring. I especially like that she's a maple and so related, albeit loosely, to the Holloway sycamore. Although she will always be tiny in comparison to her fellow maples, I re-pot her religiously and dream of a day when she might be big enough to have whirligigs of her own.

ANOTHER MAPLE WORTH KNOWING

First introduced to the UK in the seventeenth century, the Norway maple (*Acer platanoides*) and its cultivars are regularly selected for city life, be it park or street, because they tolerate compacted soil and pollution well. It's similar to the sycamore, and it can be tricky to tell the two apart. There are some key differences, though, including that the Norway maple is smaller, its clusters of flowers are upright rather than drooping, and its bark is pale and ridged, not scaled.

The oaks

There are 500 different types of oak tree. There are evergreen oaks that keep their leaves all year round, and there are deciduous oaks that lose their foliage in winter. Their leaves vary from familiarly scalloped ones to those looking a lot like holly. But all oaks have one thing in common: the acorn, a small egg-like nut sitting inside a tiny cup. The oak is also one of the few trees you might actually know the taste of – its wood is used to make the barrels in which wine, sherry, whisky and bourbon are flavoured and aged.

COMMON OAK
Quercus robur

'*Robur*' speaks of this tree's robustness, strength and power. Alternative common names include 'English oak' and 'pedunculate oak' – 'peduncle' meaning stalk and acknowledging the fact that this particular oak's acorn is displayed on the end of a long one.

Shape is very various and branches zigzag; can become massive and gnarled with age. (Fig. 43)

Leaves are smooth and green with a wavy edge. (Fig. 44)

Bark is greyish-brown and vertically ridged.

Flowers are yellow-green drooping catkins (male), hard-to-see reddish spires (female), both on the same tree.

Fruit are glossy brown acorns, growing in small clusters on long stalks. (Fig. 45)

Found in urban and peri-urban parks and woods.

Fig. 43

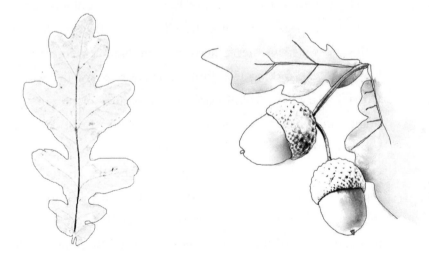

Fig. 44

Fig. 45

The oak is one of our best-loved trees, easily recognized by that most well-known of all tree nuts, the acorn, which looks like a golden egg sitting inside a scaly cup. Although it's a species strongly associated with the British countryside, the urban oak is not a rarity. In fact there are more than 900,000 oaks in Greater London alone. You'll find oak growing in parks and small city woodlands, as well as in woods on the outer edges of town. It's a tree that can live for more than five centuries, and there are thought to be 100 oaks in England that are over 800 years old. With great age come some fantastically knotty shapes, and the oak is a tree that seems to expand widthways as much as upwards. If you ever want to estimate the age of an oak, one method is to measure the girth of its trunk at chest height. One inch counts for one year, so a tree with a girth of, say, 150 inches would be 150 years old.

The common oak has curvy leaves with a scalloped edge. Its branches zigzag, forming fractal patterns that recall river basins, vein systems, nerve networks, the brain. Scientists have long used the forking tree form to make sense of the world. Charles Darwin's evolutionary line diagrams organized our origins into distinctly tree-like shapes, while Ernst Haeckel used various 'Trees of Life' to demonstrate how everything is connected. Today, biologists use 'phylogenetic trees' to represent the evolutionary relationships between organisms. It's not quite the same thing, but neuroscientist Santiago Ramón y Cajal's pioneering investigations into the microscopic structure of the brain resulted in hundreds of drawings that look uncannily oak-like. To me, his illustrations make trees and people seem at one, if only in the shared patterns of our make-up.

Once of vital practical importance to Britain's ship-building industry, the oak has been of spiritual importance for even longer. It was the sacred tree of both Zeus and Thor, while in Celtic mythology the oak was seen as a gateway between worlds. The oak's shape, its longevity and its deep history mean that we choose it to join us at key moments in our lives. This was true in the past and it's still true today. Two of my friends married their partners underneath ancient oaks – trees big enough to embrace family and friends. Another planted a young oak to mark the birth of her son, burying the placenta in the earth beneath it, where it would break down and nourish the tree's roots.

::::

To learn more about the common oak and the urban places where it currently thrives, I head south of the river. Before it was suburban, south London was wildwood, an area that in Anglo-Saxon times became known as the Great North Wood. Little of that survives, but Dulwich and Sydenham Hill Woods make up the largest remaining fragment of what was once a vast oak and hornbeam forest. The oak trees were important to London's tanning industry, which was focused around Bermondsey, close to the Thames. Oak bark contains tannins: bitter, astringent chemicals that the tree produces to defend itself from chewing insects. As well as being antioxidant, which means they can reduce cell damage, tannins bind proteins and pull animal membranes tightly together, and can be used to turn hides into leather. By the 1790s the riverside borough of Bermondsey was using the Great North Wood's tannin-rich oaks to produce one-third of the country's leather. It was a dirty, stinking, bloody process. The journalist and author of *London Labour and the London Poor*, Henry Mayhew wrote of Bermondsey in 1850, 'A walk through the streets and roads of that district is sufficient to convince three of the senses – the sight, the smell and the hearing – how extensive is this branch of industry. On every side are seen announcements of the carrying on of the leather trade; the peculiar smell of raw hides and skins, and of tan pits, pervades the atmosphere, and the monotonous click of the steam engines used in grinding bark assails the ear.' Some of the tannery buildings are still standing, although the industry left the inner city long ago. Other commercial activities in the Great North Wood included charcoal production, and coppicing for poles and posts. What remains of the forest today is managed as a nature reserve, and together Dulwich and Sydenham Hill Woods offer city dwellers twenty-five hectares of woodland retreat.

On an extremely hot day in London, what I notice most about Sydenham Hill Wood is how much cooler it is inside than out. The most welcome thing trees can offer during a heatwave is shade. I walk, aiming for an old railway tunnel where I'm to meet Daniel Greenwood, the aptly named warden of this wood. I'm pleased to be here and amble along gaily for a while, until I realize I'm lost and am going to be late. As my amble turns into a stumble, the temperature suddenly, dramatically drops. It was cool already in comparison to the streets, but now I've crossed some unseen threshold and the air has, out of nowhere, become eerily fridge-like and damp. Despite myself, I begin to panic. It is unexpected atmospheric shifts such as this that have made the woods a popular home for ill-willed, mythical beings, be it the Big Bad Wolf or the Blair Witch. I steel my nerves and try to think. Either I'm about to be picked off by something evil hiding in the bushes or I've already found my way to the Crescent Wood tunnel. It's with genuine relief that I spot Daniel, welcoming me cheerily to the coolest place in all of south London. He also reveals that, rather than housing anything creepy, the abandoned railway tunnel is protected as a hibernation roost for colonies of pipistrelle and brown long-eared bats.

Daniel grew up in this part of London, but didn't know Sydenham Hill Wood existed until he was in his twenties. It was after studying film that he realized he wanted a job where he could be outside most of the time, instead of indoors with his eyes glued to a screen. He volunteered in the nature reserve for eighteen months, before being appointed by London Wildlife Trust as its warden. He follows in a long line – there's evidence that there has been a warden of this wood since the 1200s. Daniel says he feels a sense of responsibility for it, rather than any kind of ownership.

I ask what being an urban woodland warden entails. Daniel says it's mostly about managing the public, which includes contending with antisocial behaviour, especially dog shit. As well as being unpleasant to step in, faeces and urine put a lot of nitrogen into the soil, which causes nettles and ivy to run riot. But he also relies on walkers to help him out, mentioning one local woman in particular who keeps him well informed about tawny owls, which are known to breed in the wood. Daniel's years here have taught him two crucial things about urban trees. First, that people have to be at the heart of efforts to conserve them – it was people who stopped this wood being cleared for development in the 1980s, and it's people, including numerous volunteers, who have made it what it is today. The second thing is that soil is of supreme importance. Numbers of visitors have rocketed over the last few years, and while it's great that so many want to spend time here, extra pairs of feet have had a noticeable impact on the ground. Erosion and compaction are bad for trees, as it makes it harder for their roots to breathe, and for them to take up minerals and water from the soil. Routes through the wood have to be managed, if the foundations of this ancient habitat are to be protected.

:::::

It may seem like inconsequential matter, just dirt even, but soil really is the stuff of life. It's a medium in which to grow food and fibres, it stores carbon and water, and it physically holds infrastructure in place, including our cities and towns. Trees rely on soil as much as we do. A teaspoon of rich soil contains up to one billion bacteria, within a complex and shifting mixture of grains, pores, channels and chambers. These microbes store, transform and release the nutrients that plants need to grow:

nitrogen for leaves, phosphorus for roots, potassium for flowers and fruits. Tiny animals found in the soil – creatures like beetle mites, springtails and pseudocentipedes – are a vital first link in the food chain, what author and forester Peter Wohlleben calls 'terrestrial plankton'.

Because it's out of view, it can be hard to imagine the dramas playing out beneath our feet, but plant scientists are discovering just how busy soil can be. Tree roots have been found to have a symbiotic relationship with tiny fungi called mycorrhizae, which help trees drink up essential nutrients from the earth. In exchange for sugar produced by the tree during photosynthesis, the fungi search the soil for minerals, sourcing food by breaking up tiny pebbles and rocks and ingesting that terrestrial plankton. A Radiolab documentary, *From Tree to Shining Tree*, includes a visit to an oak tree in the New York Botanical Garden in the Bronx. A soil sample from around this urban oak's roots is taken, and in it there are masses of thin, white fungal threads, each one a tenth the width of an eyelash. We learn that when times are good, a tree can bank sugar in these fungi, depositing it for future use. And because they're all linked underground by their finely intertwined fungal filaments, this sugar can also be loaned to neighbouring trees in times of need, including ones of different species. Chemical messages, including warnings and cries for help, can be shared between connected trees in the same way. They do it without voice or gesture, but, underground, trees are communicating and cooperating via what scientists have dubbed 'the wood wide web'.

It's unclear how isolated individuals operate, but it's safe to assume they're not able to enjoy the benefits of networked communal living, although they also don't have to share. Interestingly, in *Trees & Woodland in the British Landscape*, historian Oliver Rackham says the recipe for long life in an oak is that it should 'grow in a non-woodland site with plenty of room, on poor soil'. Single, so-called specimen trees are sometimes dismissed as inferior to their woodland cousins, but Rackham concludes that parkland oaks can be 'astonishingly tenacious'.

Daniel knows such oaks and tells me about one growing in nearby Dulwich Park, which has recently lost a few large limbs. One of the fallen branches has been left to decay rather than tidied up, so that the nutrients stored in it can gradually return to the soil. Daniel explains that this tree has done something remarkable, although not unheard of among oaks. It has put out tentacle-like aerial roots so that it can feed on its own decaying branch above ground, and thus reroute the nutrients from the lost limb back into itself. An oak growing aerial roots is called 'adventitious' in botany, meaning that the plant is developing structures in unexpected places, usually due to stress. Oak roots are, as a rule, below ground, and so an aerial one is decidedly unusual. Feeding on itself like this could be called auto-cannibalism of a kind, although all plants ultimately eat themselves. Rotten leaves, fruits, nuts and wood are key to the creation of healthy soil. The Dulwich oak's eccentric behaviour seems nothing but wise.

As well as feeding the tree and the earth around it, the fallen branch will also provide food and shelter for creatures like stag beetles, which rely on dead wood. Daniel points out that such saproxylic invertebrates are Europe's most threatened species group, due to changes in woodland management and the loss of ancient trees. Dead wood is therefore a hugely important resource. In both life and death, an oak like this one in Dulwich will support a phenomenal range of other living things. Home to everything from fungi, moss and lichen to small mammals and birds, the oak is the urban tree that can readily be likened to a town or a city in its own right. These relationships aren't one way, either, with the tree simply acting as a benevolent host. Oaks need visitors, not least to help ensure the next generation germinates. Squirrels and jays are our chief oak planters, burying acorns far and wide, and so helping the tree to spread.

::::

As Daniel and I have talked, we've walked, exploring his woodland workplace, before finally coming to a bench in a small clearing, oaks and hornbeams ringed around us. Their lush summer canopies cushion us from the sounds of the surrounding city, as well as shading us from the worst of the sun. It's peaceful, the trees are pacific, but the glade is also fizzing with life. It reminds me of a section in Thomas Hardy's *The Woodlanders* where Fitzpiers retreats to a part of the wood where the trees are mainly oaks: 'It was a calm afternoon, and there was everywhere around that sign of great undertakings on the part of vegetable nature.' Daniel shares Fitzpiers' awe of the natural world, and is grateful that the woods are his office. As with all offices, however, work must go on. He wishes me well, then disappears back into the trees, a man as vital to the oaks as the soil, the squirrels and the jays.

OTHER OAKS WORTH KNOWING

In America, the autumn foliage of the red oak (*Quercus rubra*) burns orange and scarlet, but in the UK fading leaves tend to turn a less eye-catching orange-brown. They're still as prettily shaped. While the edge of the common oak's leaf is scalloped, the red oak's has sharply pointed peaks and curved troughs. The red oak's acorn is different too: its cup is noticeably more shallow. And where the common oak's profile is zigzagging and rugged, the red oak's is straighter and smarter. Other oaks you'll see around town include the holm oak (*Quercus ilex*), which is an evergreen with holly-like leaves, and the pin oak (*Quercus palustris*), which has deeply indented leaves with pin-like tips that turn bright red in autumn.

The pines

There are around 100 different species of pine tree. All of them are evergreen, resinous and cone-bearing, with needle-like leaves. Pines are gymnosperms, which means they don't produce flowers and their seeds are unenclosed. These pine nuts are a key ingredient in pesto – twenty species produce nuts large enough to be harvested. Pines can be extremely long-lived, with some reaching ages well into their thousands. There's a bristlecone pine in California known as Methuselah that is thought to be 4,600 years old.

MARITIME PINE
Pinus pinaster

'*Pinus*' means ship, mast and oar, as well as pine. It's also thought to have roots in another word, meaning resin.

Shape is tall and leaning, with a broad crown that sits high up the trunk. (Fig. 46)

Leaves are pairs of long, stiff, grey-green needles, growing in exuberant tufts. (Fig. 47)

Bark is reptilian, dirty dark orange or purplish, developing deep cracks.

Fruit are small seeds, or pine nuts, held within large, slender reddish-brown cones. (Fig. 48)

Found beside the seaside, including in Bournemouth.

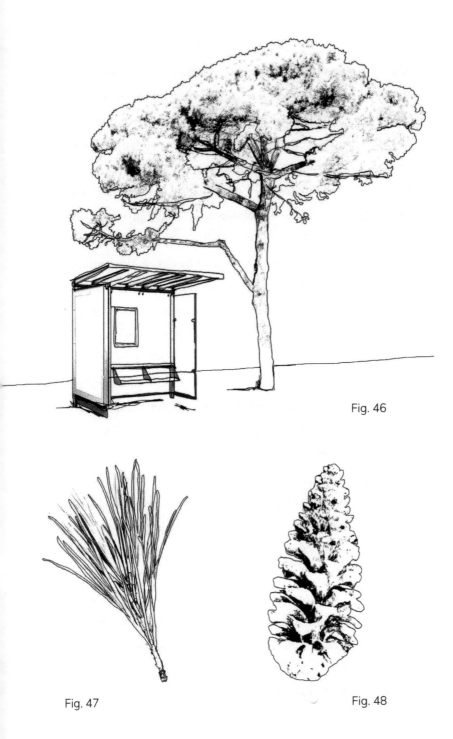

Fig. 46

Fig. 47

Fig. 48

Like the rest of the trees in its genus, the maritime pine is an evergreen and so keeps its needle-like leaves all year round. These needles are long and always grow in pairs. They contain a kind of organic antifreeze and are coated with a protective wax, which means they can survive harsh, wintry conditions, which a deciduous tree's tender leaves cannot. The maritime pine is also a conifer – or cone-bearing tree – producing the sort of woody fruits that you may well have spray-painted silver at some point, to celebrate Christmas. The cones, although narrow, can be fifteen centimetres long and may remain on the tree for several years. This pine grows tall and usually poker-straight, but sometimes at a wild angle. Low branches are rare, and its canopy balances high up its bare trunk, like a bird's nest atop a ship's mast. The bark becomes increasingly rough and reptilian with age, the sort of coarse tree skin that it's tempting to run your hands over. It's statuesque, in a scruffy sort of way, with a whiff of the prehistoric about it.

As its name suggests, the maritime pine is a tree of coastal areas. Despite being most frequently encountered in the Mediterranean, it has such a strong association with one English seaside town that it's also known in the UK as the 'Bournemouth pine'. Following the land-grabs that were made possible by the Enclosure Acts – which saw common land taken out of collective ownership and management, and handed over to private individuals – what became Bournemouth began developing on the Dorset coast in the early 1800s. A sparsely populated area, where the soil was poor and the living far from easy, was transformed within just a few decades. Villas and guest houses with ocean views were built, and once-common heathland used for grazing and turf-cutting was planted with fashionable, fast-growing conifers. In his 1841 book, *The Spas of England and Principal Sea-Bathing Places*, Augustus Granville described Bournemouth as 'a perfect discovery among the sea nooks', with fir plantations that give off 'balsamic and almost medicinal emanations'. Granville's enthusiasm for the place inspired more and more people to visit. Picture postcards from the time show the pier busy with promenaders, the men wearing boaters, the women carrying parasols. By the 1870s Bournemouth was booming, marketed as a health resort where Victorians could retreat to enjoy restorative gulps of pine-scented sea air. Famous consumptives who came to Bournemouth included an ailing Robert Louis Stevenson and, later, a young D. H. Lawrence. The health-giving evergreens had become central to the town's appeal.

There are good reasons why we find the scent of pine invigorating and therapeutic, and why we choose it for air fresheners and cleaning products. Young needles are thought to give off phytoncides, which are antimicrobial and help keep the air germ-free. And pines, like many conifers, produce a treacly liquid that the trees use to defend themselves from predators, pests and diseases. This resin can be extracted and used as turpentine, a solvent found in some oil-based paints and furniture waxes, while aromatic pine oil is used as an ingredient in several disinfectants. It also has health-improving properties. In *Tree Medicine*, Peter Conway suggests adding a few drops of warming pine oil to a bath to help release muscle tension, but also advises that it's best not to have a pine bath just before bed, as its energizing effects could keep you awake.

⸭

Bournemouth remains an attractive, coniferous retreat, popular with students and retired folk. It keeps missing out on city status, but it's still one of the largest settlements in the area, and so it had to be to there that I travelled to spend time with some urban pines. I see my first from the train between Brockenhurst and Bournemouth, standing darkly among the deciduous trees. It's an early autumn landscape, one that's starting to fade and thin, and the dark-velvet evergreens loom large among their threadbare neighbours.

The train pulls into the station and I walk into town through sleepy, leafy streets where rust-coloured pine needles carpet the pavement and car-crushed pine cones litter the roads. The sun has come out after a damp morning, and the air is warm and fragrant. Some of the street pines are typically upright poles, while others have dramatic leans, or knots and bends that look like elbows and knees. One of the maritime pines is growing at an eleven o'clock angle, straight through a garden fence, which has been cut away to accommodate its trunk. It's stretching up and out over the road, where its tousled canopy has taken on the shape of a wind-blown umbrella. I keep walking, trusting myself to be able to find the sea. I've arrived with no real plan, other than to follow my nose and see what I can find. For once, my poor sense of direction works in my favour: every wrong turn is rewarded with more pine trees.

After a brief and unpleasant encounter with a busy A-road, I head down some steep steps and into a narrow park that is bristling with conifers, as well as other broadleaved trees. I eat lunch beside a twin-trunked pine that I stare at long enough to see a face take shape in the bark. It has a round chin, a downturned mouth, sucked-in lips and a bored, unimpressed look in its half-closed eye. Seeing faces like this in abstract mediums is called 'pareidolia', which – like 'paranoid' – comes from the ancient Greek '*para*', meaning 'beyond', plus '*eidolon*', meaning 'form'. It's the word that describes what happens when we lie back on a summer's day and see animals in the clouds. If our retina records a confusing pattern, our brain scrambles around, to work out what it is. One way it does this is by making predictions based on past experiences and then projecting them onto what we see. Often those predictions are faces; we're hard-wired to see faces more than anything else, probably for good evolutionary reasons. Mistakenly seeing a face in a tree is better than missing a predator in the bushes.

When I finally reach the sea, I walk under the pier and head west. All the seaside paraphernalia is present: ice-cream sellers, amusement arcades, adventure playgrounds, even a funicular trolleying to and from a clifftop hotel. The bluffs are low, steep and gorsey, with the occasional dwarf-sized pine that's been weather-beaten into a bush. And then there are the chines. These are steep-sided, narrow valleys running away from the beach, which in Bournemouth are well wooded. Chines are found along eroding coastlines, typically in the soft sands and gravels of southern England, cut out of the earth by fast-flowing streams.

I'm tempted to walk up Alum Chine, possibly because I've read somewhere that Robert Louis Stevenson wrote *Strange Case of Dr Jekyll and Mr Hyde* while living in Skerryvore Cottage (no longer standing) on Alum Chine Road. A noticeboard explains that the chine gets its name from a short-lived attempt to mine and manufacture alum and copperas here during the late sixteenth century. Alum was used as a fixative in the dyeing process, while copperas was a dye used to make black ink. On what was originally heathland, the present mixture of deciduous and evergreen woodland was planted during the late nineteenth and early twentieth centuries.

It's bright on the beach, but gloomy in the chine – that deep, dark conifer shade. There are some large solitary pines, and other places where they're huddled together in small groups. Up ahead, a footbridge connects a road that runs along either side of the valley. The road is completely concealed by foliage, so the bridge looks as though it's suspended in mid-air among the treetops. I climb up some steep steps to get to it, which induces mild vertigo, but a little light stomach-flipping is worth it to see the pines from this new perspective. From the bridge, it's possible to look at their canopies much more closely and get a keener sense of their height. There's something of the bottle brush about a lot of them.

The climb up and over the bridge, and then the short loop

back along the road, ends with a fantastic view out over the bay, and then a steep descent past more pines back to the beach. I eat an ice cream and stare out to sea, hypnotized by the tide and the now-rhythmic throbbing of my feet. It's later I learn that the pines' presence here isn't universally welcomed. As it has been developed for housing and forestry, the area's bare heathland habitat has become rare. This is bad news for the unique wildlife that heath can support, which in this instance includes all six species of reptile found in the UK: sand lizard, common lizard, slow worm, smooth snake, adder and grass snake. The problem is that pines are exceptionally efficient at dispersing their seed and quickly take over urban heaths, if their populations aren't managed. To that end, RSPB Arne organizes an annual pull-a-pine event in neighbouring Purbeck, where around 2,500 people remove a pine each year and take it home for Christmas.

Heathland isn't important just for reptiles. Nine-mile-long Bournemouth Bay is gloriously sandy because of heath erosion, and invading pines put down roots that stop erosion taking place. Two of Bournemouth's iconic features – its green velvet pines and its fine golden sands – are in conflict then, or at least there's a delicate equilibrium between the two that has to be actively maintained.

⁘

The conifer controversy is bigger than Bournemouth. Plantation forestry began in earnest in Britain in the 1800s, including the afforestation of open heaths and moors. In 1919, at a point when the UK had less than 5 per cent tree cover – it's currently 13 per cent – the government set up the Forestry Commission, which began planting fast-growing conifers on a mass scale. In the 1950s and 1960s some of our oldest woods were destroyed with chemicals related to the notorious Agent Orange – a herbicide used to devastating effect to defoliate rural and forested areas during the Vietnam War – so that the land could become commercial conifer plantations. In the fifty years from 1933 to 1983, almost half of the UK's ancient semi-natural woodland was lost.

Many of these conifer plantations are monocultures, in private ownership and inaccessible. They have also become synonymous with tax-dodging and the super-rich, because forests that are managed commercially for timber are exempt from Inheritance and Capital Gains Tax. Pine is now one of the world's most significant trees for timber and pulp, used to create building materials and paper, but it's fair to say that tree-planting isn't always a straightforwardly positive thing. Mass afforestation of the coniferous kind can disrupt ecosystems and wipe out the wildlife that relied on what was there before.

Bournemouth's wooded chines and old town pines are full of character and charm, and it would be a poorer place without them. Unlike their more rural counterparts, urban trees are generally accessible to all, and the pines I saw on my visit were part of mixed woody areas, not monocultures. But Bournemouth's pines are also a window onto the complexities of urban conservation, and of forestry more widely, and show that tree-planting has consequences: bad as well as good.

ANOTHER CONIFER WORTH KNOWING

The dawn redwood (*Metasequoia glyptostroboides*) was introduced to Europe in the 1940s. Fast-growing, easy to propagate and instantly popular, it has spread rapidly. It has a spongy trunk with lots of vertical folds in it, with bark the colour of Irn-Bru. The dawn redwood's conical canopy will make you think of Christmas. Its needles are flat, short and soft, and its small, oval cones balance on the end of long stalks. Unusually for a conifer, it's deciduous, losing its leaves in autumn and regrowing them in spring. The redwoods include some of the world's tallest living organisms, with some species known to reach more than 115 metres high. So, although it can grow to be fifty metres tall, the dawn redwood is actually one of the smallest of the redwood trees.

The planes

The planes form a small group of tall, fast-growing, ornamental and shade-giving trees. All have lobed, palmate leaves and globular flower balls that are pollinated by the wind. Once they've set seed, these decorative balls remain on the tree throughout autumn and winter. Plane trees' most distinguishing feature is their flaky, mottled skin. There's a German camouflage pattern known as '*Platanenmuster*' that is inspired by, and named after, the plane bark's unmistakable patchwork print.

LONDON PLANE

Platanus × *hispanica*

'*Platanus*' possibly comes from an earlier word meaning broad, while '*hispanica*' refers to the fact that this tree was brought to the UK from Spain in the seventeenth century.

Shape is tall and broad, although regularly pollarded into knuckle-like shapes. (Fig. 49)

Leaves are shiny and maple-like, with five pointed lobes. (Fig. 50)

Bark is a patchy, multicoloured camouflage print of pale yellows, greens and browns.

Flowers are burgundy balls on long stalks.

Fruit are small seeds stuffed inside those now-brown balls. (Fig. 51)

Found in cities across Europe, including the English capital and Milton Keynes.

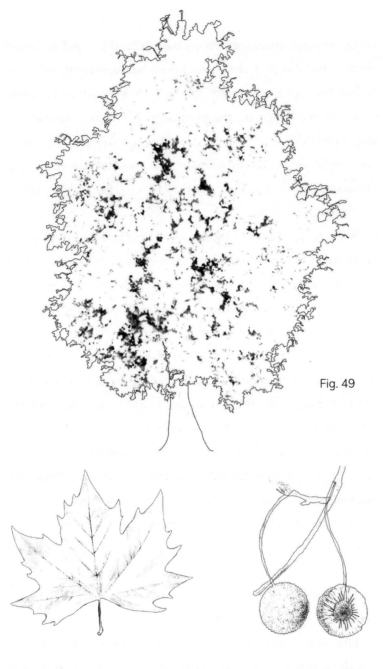

Fig. 49

Fig. 50

Fig. 51

Once autumn arrives in the sylvan city, the wind becomes blustery and damp. Tired leaves bruise banana-yellow and dirty umber, then give up entirely, spiralling downwards and coming to rest in wet heaps on the pavement. It's sepia overhead and slippery underfoot. This is the season when a single leaf, a large one, might get caught by a malevolent gust and slap you full in the face and then cling there, limp and loamy, before you, feeling humiliated, peel it off.

When Peter Ackroyd explained in *London, The Biography* that the plane tree is the reason why the capital has been apostrophized as a 'City of Trees' with 'solemn shapes' and 'glooms Romantic', I can't help but think of this time of year, when dusk descends around four o'clock in the afternoon and the first fogs of the season start to seep in. In the right light – that special tawny twilight that you sometimes get, which is a mixture of old-fashioned street lamp and wet smog – the plane trees loom, and their bulk can seem threatening or protective, depending on how your day has panned out. Some of London's planes have grown giant, while others have been shorn into mean knuckles and fists. This tree has flaky bark that's smooth but mottled. As old skin breaks away, fresh young skin is exposed underneath. The result is an irregular patchwork of greys, pistachios, ochres and olives. The plane's leaves are similar to the maple, with five pointed lobes, and it has globular flowers that set seed in autumn. These brown orbs hang on the bare tree throughout winter, festive and bauble-like.

The planes are indeed an essential part of my home town's moody romance and, perversely, it is in autumn that they really come to life. Welcome background in the summer, it's now that the trees make their presence felt by dumping their yellowed leaf load onto the street. Trees do this in order to survive freezing conditions when food and water become scarce. In *The Ash and the Beech*, Richard Mabey points out that autumn is actually 'a time of furious activity by trees, the opposite of the slow winding down or senility of hibernation', as there is so much to do in preparation for the onset of winter. Like all deciduous trees, the plane breaks down chlorophyll and sugars in its leaves and draws them into its woody parts. It then sheds them to prevent water loss, and to rid itself of the waste products and toxins it has built up over the course of the year. Being free of leaves also makes the plane more able to withstand violent winter storms. A tree in full leaf is in more danger of being swept over in high winds.

::::

While they are an essential part of the English capital's character, or the way some of us like to characterize it at least, the plane is actually not even close to being London's most common tree. There are 121,000 in Greater London, out of an estimated 8.4 million trees. The London plane is not exclusive to the capital, either. It's been a favourite of tree-planters for hundreds of years and is found in cities across the UK and beyond, chosen because it somehow seems to thrive in stressful urban environments. When the architects designing Milton Keynes in the early 1970s were choosing trees for the city's main street – a two-kilometre-long boulevard that frames the rising midsummer sun – it was the London plane to which they turned.

People can be dismissive about Milton Keynes, disliking the fact that it was designed and built from scratch, rather than evolving organically over time, and unimpressed that a grid system was favoured over a typically British warren of streets. But whatever you think of it, an urban tree-lover can't fail to be impressed by the numbers: marketed from the start as a low-rise city of trees, Milton Keynes now has twenty-two million trees and shrubs. Its cathedral is made of trees, not stone. I arrive in town with an open mind, having read a brilliant article by Patrick Barkham called 'The struggle for the soul of Milton Keynes', in which he reveals the city's architects to be 1960s dreamers, inspired by 'Stonehenge, the pyramids, ley lines'. I'm ready to respond to the place-makers' utopian visions.

The station is on the bottom level of a large mirror-glass building, and the concourse outside has the look and feel of an airport at 4 a.m. I walk across the car park and onto a paved walkway, heading east up the grid's central horizontal axis. The promise that it would be leafy is kept. There are trees and bushes everywhere, planted formally and in family groups. Midsummer Boulevard is designed to be the province of cars, not people on foot, but it is here that the planes are planted. Hundreds of them – all around the same size and shape – are growing close together in uniform rows on either side of the road and in the central reservation. They're still young and slender, and it's hard to imagine how well they will age, packed together as tightly as this.

They're nothing like London's centuries-old planes, but the tree-planters' intentions were probably similar in both cities, and the fruits of their labour will be born long after their deaths. I walk among the planes for a while – the ground around their bases is hard and compact, the unfortunate fate of all street trees – but feel myself being subtly directed away from the road and onto the pedestrian-only walkway instead.

It's Saturday, but it's quiet, hardly anyone about. The walkway runs parallel to Midsummer Boulevard, a car park now between me and the planes. At regular intervals the footpath passes under roads that are following the vertical axis. I climb up, so I can look both ways down one of them, and I see that it's a wide boulevard lined with horse chestnuts. The underpasses are open and airy, and in almost all of them is at least one tent, sometimes two or three. The people living in them seem to have systems in place, their gear organized neatly into shopping crates and trolleys, and it looks like they've been camping out here for a while. I don't see anyone, though, just a single pair of feet sticking out of a zipped-up tent door.

I keep walking. Midsummer Boulevard comes to an abrupt end in the face of a large shopping centre. Two planes stand sentry in front of it. Behind the trees is a concrete disc painted egg-yolk yellow, in homage to the sun. I continue straight ahead, through the shopping centre, out the other side, through another car park, across some roads and into Campbell Park. Formal at first, it slowly loosens up and starts to feel wilder, with grass left long and wildflowers allowed to grow. There are stands of mature trees here that pre-date the city. I cross the Grand Union Canal, which is screened by Lombardy poplars, walk through a bit more parkland and finally arrive at the Tree Cathedral. Its environs are currently being used as a green burial site for the scattering and interment of ashes, as well as functioning as a park. There are rose petals, broken glow sticks and burned-out candles on the ground, remnants of a recent parting. It's hushed and peaceful inside, although you never quite forget that this cathedral has been exiled to the edge of the city and sandwiched between some busy roads and a theme park.

Hornbeam and lime trees form the nave, with the hornbeams making up the central avenue through the space. The trees touch, forming a holloway-like tunnel. Evergreens represent the central tower and spire, and the chapels are marked out by cherries. Every tree is carefully placed, planted to mimic the shape and scale of Norwich Cathedral. In *The Tree*, John Fowles argues that all sacred buildings, whatever beliefs they serve, replicate to some extent the aura of woodland or forest settings. Trees, 'blind, immobile, speechless', are the 'only form a universal god could conceivably take'.

I walk back to the station, taking a slightly different route through the park and the city, but following another horizontal axis nonetheless. Milton Keynes isn't my kind of place, I decide, too suburban and quiet and controlled. Too new. For now. Milton Keynes' trees were all planted around the same time, and the whole place, including its vegetation, has a uniformity that I find odd. But it is a good example of how trees can be designed into a city's make-up – more towns should be as forested as this one. In a hundred years, if they make it, the midsummer planes will surely have outgrown their current neat perfection and will have attained silhouettes suitably romantic and solemn.

ANOTHER TOUGH STREET TREE WORTH KNOWING

In the face of a disease that's seen thousands of the Canal du Midi's planes felled in France, tree officers here have to think about what might come next. The American sweet gum (*Liquidambar styraciflua*) is a popular choice, not least because it's considered to be climate-change resilient and therefore future-proof. It has a domed shape and striking star-shaped leaves that flush scarlet in autumn, as well as corky bark and decorative spiky fruits. Many different ornamental varieties exist. The tree's botanical name, *Liquidambar*, describes the aromatic gum it produces. Also known as 'storax' and 'copalm balsam', this gum is used to scent incense, perfume, balms and ointments.

The poplars

There are thirty-five different types of poplar tree and almost all are either male or female, never both. The male trees sport long catkins in early spring, while pollinated females go on to produce tiny fruits that are protected by a cotton-wool-like down. The ground beneath a fruiting female looks as if it has been dusted with snow, and the air around her is foggy with fluff.

BLACK POPLAR
Populus nigra betulifolia

'*Betulifolia*' reveals that this tree has foliage similar to a birch. Poplars are also known as cottonwood trees because of the fluffy down produced by fruiting females.

Shape is large and lumpish, with a distinct lean to one side. (Fig. 52)

Leaves are yellow-green, toothed and teardrop-shaped; quivery in the lightest breeze. (Fig. 53)

Bark is darkest brown-black and deeply fissured.

Flowers are long, reddish-brown catkins (male), strings of tiny green beads (female), on separate trees. (Fig. 54)

Fruit are small capsules surrounded by an abundance of woolly white fluff.

Found in streets, parks and herbariums; once common up north, now rare.

Fig. 52

Fig. 53

Fig. 54

I meet my first black poplar on Oxford Road, outside Manchester University Hospital and opposite the Whitworth Museum. It's a large tree growing behind shoulder-high railings. The trunk is bulky but twiggy, and leaning subtly to the left, with black bark that is rough-hewn and igneous-looking. Overhead, the tree's yellow-green leaves flutter gently. Each is wide at the base, pointed at the tip, teardrop-shaped and toothed, similar to birch but bigger. This particular poplar is near-neighbour to an ash, and their frothy canopies have mingled in the sky.

The variety of black poplar that is also known as the 'Manchester poplar' was planted in the city for good reason from the mid-1800s onwards. As a beating heart of Britain's Industrial Revolution, Manchester was a filthy city, a place where wildlife struggled to survive. In the 1850s it was said that a pine would die within three miles of Manchester Town Hall, and even the London plane, that tree of tolerance, struggled to stand the city's acrid air. But somehow the black poplar could, and it became a popular choice for Victorian tree-planters. Later, during the Depression of the 1930s, a job-creation scheme saw men being trained to take black-poplar cuttings. They were each given a bicycle and a tree-planting pin and sent off to spread young poplars across the city. So, because of terrible pollution and an almighty financial crash, Manchester has been gifted with the highest concentration of black poplars anywhere in the UK, albeit a number that is rapidly diminishing.

Propagating trees from cuttings is cheap and effective, but it creates clones that are genetically identical. The majority of the poplars planted in the city are thought to have come from a single male tree, a conscious decision so as to avoid having to clean up the woolly cotton-wool-like fluff produced by fruiting females. Planting clones is always a risk. Without diversity, if one tree is hit by disease, the whole lot could be wiped out. The most recent black-poplar biodiversity action plan for Greater Manchester estimated the population to be around 5,000–7,000 in 2000, with trees being 'found across the conurbation with the greatest concentrations in the east and north where airborne pollution was at its worst and the highest concentration of nineteenth-century industry was found'. Just five years later, in 2005, almost half of these poplars were dead, felled because of a disease caused by the poplar scab, *Venturia populina*.

The Oxford Road poplar that I'm standing beside cuts a lonely figure. The area is leafy, full of majestic ashes and mighty planes, but there's not another poplar in sight, on the street or in the Whitworth's wooded park. However, up the road there's a captive collection. The Manchester Museum has a herbarium containing 750,000 plant specimens, including the black poplar, and the curator of botany has said she will give me a tour.

A herbarium is a methodically organized collection of dried plants, placed in a book, a room or a building, depending on the collection's size. It could be a personal project or a teaching aid, or both. Manchester Museum's herbarium is a modest one, nestled in the attic of one of the University of Manchester's grandest buildings. The main space is vaulted and light, with the feeling of a chapel as well as a classroom. There are paper pom-poms suspended from the ceiling, and wide banks of boxes, cabinets and chests stacked off to the sides. A selection of botanical models and books, and various dried twigs, leaves and fruits, are spread out on the long table that runs down the middle of the room. Rachel Webster's office is up a small set of stairs at the back and has walls painted bright lemon. It's quiet, just me and Rachel here this afternoon, although she does share the space with a couple of colleagues, as well as groups of visiting school children and volunteers.

Rachel invites me into a warren of narrow corridor rooms, each containing hundreds of identical dark-green boxes. These archive boxes protect the contents inside from sunlight, damp and insects, and each one is carefully labelled with a description of the plant it contains. We walk between rows stacked ten boxes high, before Rachel stops and slides one box out, setting it down and removing the lid. The front panel drops forward, making it easier to remove what's inside, and she lifts out some large folded pieces of paper. Within each folded sheet is another loose one with a section of plant taped or sewn to it. The plants are flat, the life squeezed out of them, and many have dried to a dull brown or grey. The specimen sheets all have notes attached, giving the plant's name, who collected it and where. Some of these labels are elaborately handwritten in ink. Rachel selects a few precious things to show me, including pressed seaweeds that have miraculously kept their purples and pinks, and some amateur albums akin to holiday scrapbooks. With every box and book she opens, I'm anticipating a smell, but it's all surprisingly odourless. She explains that most of the specimens in the herbarium date from between 1860 and 1910 and are primarily the work of three collectors, Charles Bailey, James Cosmo Melvill and Leopold Hartley Grindon.

Bailey was a Manchester businessman who decided to start his own herbarium after attending evening classes in botany. His ambition was to collect a specimen of every European plant from every country in which it grew. Melvill was a friend of Bailey, also a businessman and amateur botanist. He collected shells as well as plants, and spent a fortune buying other people's specimens, including items from the herbarium of Carl Linnaeus and plants collected by Charles Darwin on the *Beagle* voyage. Grindon is the most interesting of the three, motivated more by sharing the information he gathered. He was a teacher and writer, and used his herbarium as reference material for his classes, articles and books. He moved to Manchester from Bristol when he was twenty, and his collection includes cultivated as well as wild plants, alongside personal correspondence, printed information and illustrations clipped from magazines and books. He ran botanical courses for working men in his spare time.

Rachel has already set out the herbarium's black-poplar specimens for me on a workbench. Some sheets bear twigs with buds but no leaves, others have catkins, seeds and even the cottony fluff of the rare female tree. One sheet has nothing on it at all except specks of black-poplar dust. Some of the specimens have deepened to a rich brown-black, and there are hints of pale silver and muted gold, but most of the foliage has faded to beige. Only two are definitively marked as being 'Manchester poplar'. One dates from 21 June 1946 and has three twigs carefully taped to it. The crisp leaves have dulled to olive-brown, although the stems and veins flash orange. The other specimen dates from April 1973 and is labelled in blue biro 'Populus nigra ("Manchester Poplar"). Male trees on green in Plymouth Grove, formerly the gardens of old slum houses.' This specimen sheet has two arching twigs taped to it, both leafless but with buds.

Leopold Hartley Grindon's black-poplar box contains much more than dried twigs and leaves. It has pages ripped from journals and magazines, handwritten notes and correspondence, and woodcut illustrations cut out of books. One specimen sheet has a small hand-made envelope attached to it, which Rachel carefully opens to reveal the skeleton of a single black-poplar leaf, pressed onto a sheet of bright-blue paper. The cuticles and cells have wasted away to leave behind a teardrop of intricate bone-white filigree. Because of the choice of blue paper, the effect is like one of Victorian botanist Anna Atkins' cyanotypes – those beautiful blue-and-white early photographs of plants, which she made using a combination of chemicals and the sun.

We move off through a sea of green boxes, Rachel explaining that Manchester Museum's herbarium is now used mainly for education and public exhibitions. Bailey, Melvill and Grindon's original donations make up the bulk of the collection, but the herbarium does occasionally accept new items. She leads me up to a narrow table, which has a collection of old-fashioned microscopes on top, positioned alongside two desktop cabinets with glass doors. Behind the doors are wide, shallow drawers, each with a tiny numbered handle. Rachel pulls one out, revealing the drawer to be a velvet-lined tray of glass slides, all marked with a translucent blob of bright orange, red or pink. Selecting a slide and gripping it between forefinger and thumb, she holds it up to the light. Illuminated, it looks like a splinter from a stained-glass window. My eyes focus in on the hot-pink smear and I see that it's the slenderest slither of a tree bud. It's labelled 'Lombardy poplar'. Because of the Manchester poplar's sad demise, this is the urban poplar you'll now see the most, one that couldn't really be more different: slim where the black poplar is wide, bolt upright where the black poplar leans to one side. The delicate bud cross-section is beautiful, but bittersweet.

This place is an archive of plant matter and of the people who collected it and, I suppose, like any museum that primarily explores the past, loss can't help but be part of its make-up. Picked and preserved, the plants themselves are of course dead, and in this instance the people who did the picking and preserving are too. But collections can be more than just historical records of what we once had. The Millennium Seed Bank in Sussex is similar to a herbarium, only with its eyes firmly on the future. Seeds are collected, dried to around 4–6 per cent moisture content, then stored in deep-freeze chambers in a vast vault. Britain is the first country in the world to have preserved its botanical heritage in this way, and the seed bank is collecting samples from other countries too, aiming to have conserved 25 per cent of the world's plant species by 2020. As well as being a comprehensive record of plant life, the bank is a kind of insurance policy against extinction. In theory, and if necessary, the stored seeds can be germinated and reintroduced to the wild, or used in scientific research. It doesn't give us an excuse to be careless with what we've got, but it is reassuring to have this backup, just in case.

ANOTHER POPLAR WORTH KNOWING

The Lombardy poplar (*Populus nigra* 'Italica') is an upright – or 'fastigiate' – cultivar, with tight-packed, upswept, almost vertical branches. Introduced to Britain in 1758, it was one of the first fastigiate trees planted in the UK. It has greyish-brown bark and red catkins in spring. Its most distinguishing feature is its silhouette, which is extremely slim and spire-like, the very opposite of the Manchester poplar's broad and slanting frame. It's a tough and resilient tree, one that is planted in groups to form a disguising screen or windbreak.

The trees of heaven

There are thought to be up to ten different types of tree of heaven, although the exact number, as for other groups of trees, is in dispute. They're quick-growing and hardy, with strikingly large, ash-like leaves made up of leaflets arranged alternately along a central stem. Trees of heaven employ an antisocial strategy known as 'allelopathy' in order to squash competition, leaking toxins into the soil that stop other species from taking root.

TREE OF HEAVEN
Ailanthus altissima

'*Ailanthus*' probably has its roots in an Indonesian word meaning 'tree of the gods' or 'tree reaching for the sky'; '*altissima*' suggests something very similar: tallest, lofty, profound.

Shape is tall, wide and elegant, with upward-twisting branches. (Fig. 55)

Leaves are large and compound, made up of tapered leaflets, each with a small notch at the base. (Fig. 56)

Bark is dark grey with snaking vertical stripes.

Flowers are yellowish-white spikes; a tree can be male, female or both. (Fig. 57)

Fruit are decorative bunches of single-winged seeds, sometimes brightly coloured.

Found in inner-city estates, squares and streets.

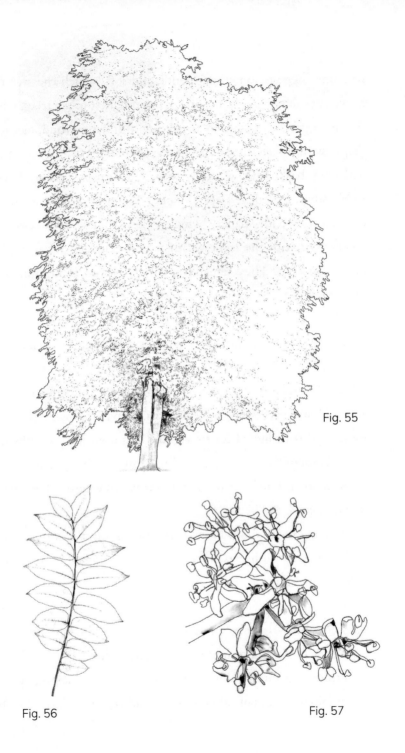

Fig. 55

Fig. 56

Fig. 57

Its name suggests something gentle and soft, which the tree of heaven absolutely is not. It's one of our toughest urban trees, well able to cope with pollution and drought. It has a proud, elegant shape, with foliage that looks like giant plumes of feathers, and dark-grey bark that's vertically striped with pale, snaking lines. In late summer, female trees produce a bounty of fruit, each seed encased in a wide, papery wing or 'key'. These keys start off green, but, with the right weather, will gradually ripen bright orange and red. They remain on the tree through autumn and winter, after the leaves have been shed.

The tree of heaven has something of the ash about it, but it's much more muscular and vigorous, with louder foliage and larger keys. It's short-lived, fast-growing and fast-spreading, producing many suckers and seedlings. Like other plants that are bold and successful, it's labelled invasive and aggressive by some, and is maligned for its vigour. It is notorious worldwide as a cosmopolitan weed tree, and is known as the 'ghetto palm' in New York City because it will grow anywhere – the more down-at-heel, the better.

Reading more about New York's urban forest, I come across Leslie Day, an author who has written about her home city's wildlife, including its trees. Not only is she interested in urban nature, she also used to live on a boat. Believing we must be kindred spirits, I strike up a conversation with her online. I learn that Leslie is a retired schoolteacher who is now studying scientific illustration. She's recently started teaching plant morphology for botanical illustrators, and says she's dazzled daily by the exquisite form and function of plant and animal parts. Leslie has moved now, but for many years she lived with her family and a menagerie of pets on a converted trawler in the 79th Street Boat Basin. It's beside Riverside Park, which runs along the Hudson River from West 65th to 155th. She describes it as a beautiful, idyllic place with views of the Upper West Side and downtown New York City.

I ask Leslie about the tree of heaven, and New Yorkers' relationship with it. 'It is a very, very common tree in New York because it grows where nothing else can,' she explains. 'It is considered a weed tree by the Parks Department but they leave it alone in neighbourhoods where it might be the only green plant giving shade and beauty. They produce thousands of seeds, which easily germinate and so they are everywhere. New Yorkers love them because it was the tree in the classic book *A Tree Grows in Brooklyn* by Betty Smith.'

My next move is, of course, to get a copy of this novel. In it I read about a girl called Francie, who spends her Saturday afternoons in summer sitting on her apartment block's fire escape, three floors up, daydreaming, ensconced in the canopy of a tree of heaven, which has foliage like 'a lot of opened green umbrellas'. It's strong-willed and 'no matter where its seed fell, it made a tree which struggled to reach the sky', even if that was on a boarded-up lot or a rubbish heap. It's the only tree Francie knows that can grow out of cement.

The tree of heaven, originally from China, has a close connection with London as well as New York. This is especially true of Bermondsey, where it was widely planted during the 1920s when the fashion for chinoiserie was at its height. The tree-planting was the work of the borough's Beautification Committee, which was spearheaded by its mayor, Ada Salter. Ada was unusual, not least because she held public office at a time when women were rarely permitted to achieve such positions of political power.

Keen to find out more about Ada Salter, I find a guided walk designed to tell her story, led by two knowledgeable women called Oona Gay and Sue McCarthy. As we set out down Bermondsey Street, I learn that Ada moved to the borough as a young woman and lived in what was known as a 'settlement', a project that planted middle-class people in poor inner-city areas to do good works. Settlements were an acceptable way for young, unmarried women to leave small towns, and their endless cycles of tea parties and church fetes, and move to the big city alone. It was in the Bermondsey settlement that Ada met Alfred Salter. They fell in love with each other, and with the borough, married and stayed in the area for the rest of their lives. Now chic and expensive, Bermondsey was industrial back then, dominated by jam factories and tanneries. In the 1910s, Ada supported striking local women workers at one of the more notorious jam factories, in their calls for more rights. A woman had died after falling into a vat of boiling apples – just one of a number of incidents that politicized Ada and pushed the workers to walk out.

Ada and Alfred later became Quakers and pacifists. The First World War was a difficult time for them. The couple supported conscientious objectors and came under fire for it from the local community. A mob even gathered outside their house one night, but Alfred managed to persuade them to leave by reminding them of all the good works he and Ada had done. Local people were swept up in war fever, but when (some of) the men returned from the front, people's views gradually changed, and the Salters' position in the community was restored. The 1920s and 1930s were good decades. Ada became Mayor of Bermondsey and Alfred was elected as an MP. It was during this time that many trees were planted across the borough, mainly flowering cherries and trees of heaven. The latter was chosen for its name as well as its good looks, the idea being to elevate and beautify Bermondsey, both physically and spiritually. Many of Ada's trees live on today.

I didn't know the tree of heaven, or Ada Salter, existed until I decided to learn more about the species around me. I now see 'ghetto palms' and Ada's beautifying influence all over my home city. There are three magnificent mature trees on my cycle route to work, as well as seedlings sprouting up in some extraordinary places close by. These saplings remind me of the butterfly bush and the sycamore – plants that people love to hate because of their persistence, but I can't help admiring. The tree of heaven has a mind of its own and, like Ada, is getting on with greening the city by itself.

ANOTHER LARGE-LEAVED EXOTIC WORTH KNOWING

The Indian bean tree (*Catalpa bignonioides*) – also known as the 'Indian cigar' and the 'smoking bean' – originates from the south-eastern United States. It takes its common names from its striking seedpods, which are slender, stick-bean-shaped and up to forty centimetres long. They remain on the tree throughout winter, hanging down like great clumps of dried brown spaghetti. The Indian bean is medium-sized, with a short trunk and a bushy, broad crown. Its bark is ridged and scaly, while its leaves are very large, rounded and vaguely heart-shaped. They're late to unfurl, and are followed by trumpet-shaped flowers that are white, splashed with purple and orange. This unusual-looking tree is occasionally found planted along city streets, but you're most likely to spot it in urban parks, arboretums and botanic gardens. There are plenty of ornamental varieties, all with showy flowers and pods.

The whitebeams

The whitebeams are so called because the undersides of their leaves are pale and felted, and their domed canopies look silvery-white when the wind blows in the right direction. Their timber is also white, as well as hard and fine-grained. These trees have clusters of cream-coloured flowers in spring, followed by red or brown berries in autumn. They're part of the large *Sorbus* genus, which also includes rowan and service trees.

BRISTOL WHITEBEAM

Sorbus bristoliensis

'*Sorbus*' stems from a word meaning red, probably in reference to the tree's berries; 'beam' means wood in Old English.

Shape is sturdy and compact, with a rounded crown; the trunk is often forked. (Fig. 58)

Leaves are lobed, dark green on top, felty grey-green underneath. (Fig. 59)

Bark is smooth and grey, cracking with age.

Flowers are small and creamy white, clustered together loosely.

Fruit are round, russet berries. (Fig. 60)

Found clinging to cliff edges on the outskirts of Bristol.

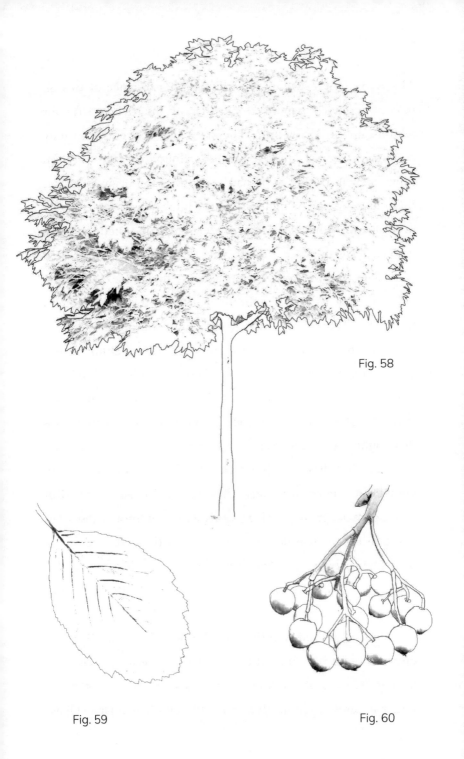

Fig. 58

Fig. 59

Fig. 60

The Avon Gorge, which is within spitting distance of Bristol, is considered by experts to be one of the richest sites for whitebeams in the world. The trees like its rocky, scrubby conditions, being unusual in their ability to take root on thin, uneven ground. The hardy Bristol whitebeam is scarce, thought to be one of eight different whitebeams that grow only in this part of England. All eight are ancient apomictic hybrids, which means their seeds don't need to be fertilized in order to germinate, and their offspring are all essentially asexual clones. How to tell a Bristol whitebeam apart from the rest requires a keen eye. Rather than white, the felt on the underside of its leaves is greenish-grey, and its trunk will often, although not always, split in two and become forked. The Bristol whitebeam population is considered to be healthy, if tiny. There are currently 306 known trees, all growing in an area that's less than eight kilometres square.

There's a disappointing lack of folklore associated with whitebeams, perhaps because they are such elusive trees. But although wild-growing whitebeams are uncommon, those of us living in urban areas do meet members of the extended family on a regular basis. The Swedish whitebeam (*Sorbus intermedia*) is the vigorous Scandinavian cousin of the rare Bristolian. It's a tough and pollution-tolerant tree that was widely planted in towns, cities and suburbs after the Second World War. It's one of those neat, compact trees that are sometimes accused of having the look of a lollipop. It has dark-green leaves that are soft, pale grey underneath and faintly oakish in shape. Dense clusters of cream flowers blanket it in spring, followed by berries that ripen to brownish-orange in late summer and autumn.

::::

An essay in an anthology called *Arboreal* gave me my first brief glimpse of the Bristol whitebeam. In 'City, Trees, Water' – three of my favourite things – author Helen Dunmore discusses the redevelopment of Bristol's docks, which she dates as beginning in the 1970s when a row of young plane trees was planted. Forty years on, the planes are magnificent and the abandoned dockland has been transformed into a luxurious harbour, with some of the raw edges left artfully intact. Dunmore lived overlooking the docks, with the Avon Gorge right there, a green gape at its side, and she knew both well. In the essay, she remarks how entrancing it is to have the gorge so close by, to have such wildness as part of her home city's 'breath and being, part of its understanding of itself'. Later, Dunmore describes taking a guided ferry trip through the gorge, revealing it to be richly wooded with 'oak, ash, birch, hazel, holly, guelder rose, yew, hawthorn, coppice hazel, small-leaved lime, dogwood and whitebeam of all kinds'.

Intrigued by the essay and the journey it describes, I book tickets to go on the same boat trip, and I invite my mum along to keep me company. Bristol is a midway point between her home in south Wales and mine in London. Unlike Helen Dunmore, who lived in Bristol for more than forty years, I don't know the city at all. For me, so far, it's been a pause on a train journey or a sign at the side of the motorway. It's the place with the bridges and the tunnels that enable you to leave one country so easily and enter another.

Mum and I meet at Temple Meads station and walk to the docks. We eat lunch in one of Bristol's many waterside cafés, before boarding the *Brigantia*. The boat is bright yellow, with room for around forty passengers, and has a large plastic Gromit the dog attached to her bow. Wallace and Gromit, a couple of cheese-loving clay film stars first brought to life by animator Nick Park, are two of Bristol's most famous creations, much better known than the rare whitebeam that has taken the city's name.

The journey begins in a lock that lowers us from the harbour's flat waters into the tidal River Avon. As a canal-boat dweller, I'm familiar with locks. The ones I know generally have space for two narrowboats just about to squeeze in side by side, and they're operated with a windlass and elbow grease. This lock is enormous in comparison, with enough room to accommodate several large boats at once. It's also fully automated, and no frantic hand-winding is required to let water in or out. We share the lock with a speedboat, a couple of rigid inflatables, another sightseeing ferry like ours and a small ship called the *Pride of Bristol*. Once we're secured to the lock sides with loose ropes and chains, the gates shut and the water quickly starts to drop, taking us down with it. The bustling harbour disappears, and for a moment our surroundings become dim and dank. And then the water stops dropping, the gate swings open and everything brightens again.

Cities tend to peter out gradually through slow-thinning suburbia and light industry, but this is an instant shift. *Brigantia* is first out and, as we motor away, we cross from one realm into another. If you looked back over your shoulder at this point you would see the city still firm on its foundations, but the eye is drawn irresistibly ahead, where there is no city at all, just a churn of brown river water and a slash of blue sky, with a mass of autumnal foliage towering up on either side. It's not just verdant, it's rocky too. The Clifton Suspension Bridge cuts across the gorge straight ahead, 245 feet up. Everyone on the boat is taking pictures, and Gromit's arse is in them all.

Somewhere out there the Bristol whitebeam resides. I quickly realize there's no way I'm going to pick one out from down here, no matter how good the binoculars I've borrowed are. The landscape changes dramatically as we head further west, flattening out and becoming more obviously peopled again, with roads, houses and boat clubs alongside the river. The focus of the ferry's wildlife-themed commentary is the Avon's birds, and together we spot gulls, grey herons, Canada geese and cormorants, and waders including redshanks, lapwings and common sandpipers. We pass a boatyard packed with vessels in varying states of collapse. The landscape becomes increasingly industrial and estuarial.

::::

Another well-known Bristolian is the artist Richard Long, whose work includes drawings, books and murals made using mud collected from this very river. He treats river mud as though it were paint – in the Avon's case, it's a soft shade of light brown – and chance, water and gravity play a key part in how his final artworks turn out. These pieces manage to be chaotic and peaceful all at once. In an interview for *The Economist* in 2008, the artist explained that 'River Avon tidal mud is unbelievably strong and viscous. It has all the natural binding qualities, like cave paintings.' A mural for Bristol's Arnolfini in 2015 saw Long use his fingers to cover the top half of a gallery wall in swirls of wet mud, before leaving it to drip down the rest. The result, to me, looks like a wind-raked waterway fringed by swaying reeds, a human- and mud-made riverscape that must contain thousands of the artist's smeared fingerprints. To someone else, it would look like something different. In that 2008 interview, Long said of his mud works that he liked the fact that 'you have the infinitesimal little splashes and drips and crosshairs of the microscale, and there's the big powerful image you can see when you stand back'.

In an article for *It's Nice That*, writer Alexander Hawkins beautifully describes Richard Long's interventions both outside and inside the gallery as 'a form of mark making that imposes human rationale on the chaos of the natural world'. Being ferried down the Avon, the wind turning my skin pink and the brackish air my hair frizzy, I imagine the artist having no time at all for narrated pleasure trips like this. Instead, Long would surely arrive at the river on foot, wading right into the mud to collect the raw materials he needs to create his work, sinking his hands deep into the cool, brown silk, a man without inhibitions about being so intimate with river or earth.

⁚⁚⁚⁚⁚

The water widens right out at Avonmouth and there's the M4 crossing the water, Wales straight ahead. It's a bridge that Mum and I both know well, although we've never seen it like this before, looking sleek and sculptural in the near-distance. *Brigantia* loops around and we head back the way we came, back through the industrial flatlands, back through the green-and-brown gorge. It is indeed part of Bristol's breath and being, and made twice as big by the mirror of the river water. And then we're back in the lock. The same boats we shared it with on the way down are reunited for the journey back up. Although we didn't see the whitebeam in person – or any land artists gathering mud – sometimes just knowing something is out there, thriving in its own niche, is enough.

ANOTHER SORBUS WORTH KNOWING

The rowan (*Sorbus aucuparia*), a small and slender tree, is also known as the mountain ash and the quickbeam. It has silvery-grey bark and cream-coloured flowers. It's a regular sight along city streets, and an attractive one in late summer and autumn when it's laden with berries that traffic-light through green and amber to festive scarlet. It has feathery leaves, each one made up of around fifteen toothed leaflets, which can flush crimson

---

before they drop. The rowan has its own mythology and was once a species considered worth planting close to home for the protection it offered from witches. According to the Woodland Trust, its old Celtic name was '*fid na ndruad*', meaning wizard's tree, while modern Druids believe it to be a portal between worlds.

The yews

Yews are some of the world's longest-lived trees. Evergreen conifers, they have soft needle-like leaves and fleshy, cup-shaped fruits that hold a toxic pip. These trees are notorious for being poisonous but potent, and are now celebrated as the source of a cancer-fighting drug.

COMMON YEW

Taxus baccata

'*Baccata*' means 'bearing red berries', while 'yew' possibly once meant brown.

Shape is broad and bushy, with low upswept branches; hollowing out with age. (Fig. 61)

Leaves are flat, soft needles; dark green on top, grey-green underneath. (Fig. 62)

Bark is dark purplish-red and flaky; it 'bleeds' when cut.

Flowers are small, round and yellow (male), tiny green buds (female), on separate trees.

Fruit is a poisonous seed, held inside a fleshy pink-red cup. (Fig. 63)

Found in graveyards, parks and botanic gardens.

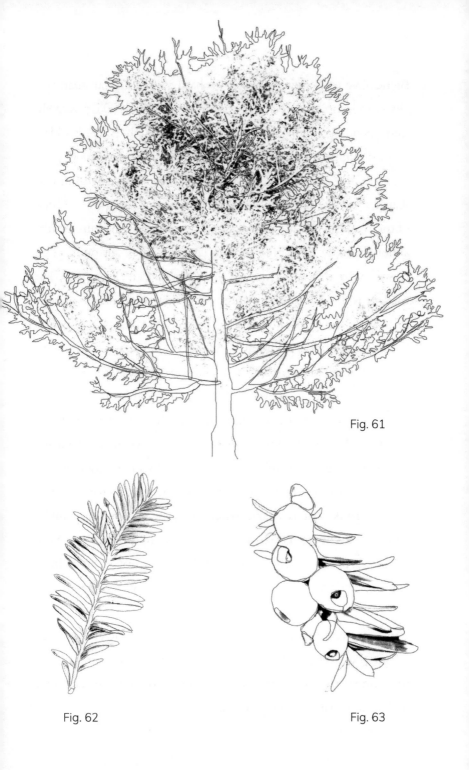

Fig. 61

Fig. 62

Fig. 63

Being alive for hundreds of years is hard to fathom, but sharing a city with something that has lived for more than 1,000 is positively mind-bending. Living to be 600 or more, with Britain's oldest yews thought to be somewhere between 2,000 and 3,000 years old, it is the common yew's longevity more than anything else that has secured its place as one of our most revered trees. Once of the woods, yews are now strongly associated with churchyards, although many trees pre-date the churches they surround. The reasons why they are found in these places aren't clear, but one rumour is that yews were planted on the graves of plague victims to protect and purify the dead. The tree's longevity has seen it become a symbol of immortality, while its sombre association with burial grounds has earned it the nickname 'the tree of the dead'.

Great age produces excellent looks, in tree terms at least. The longer-lived a tree is, the more gnarled it will become. Yews don't reach lofty heights, but they do achieve massive girths. Multi-stemmed and shrubby, low-growing branches strive up and out, while thicker limbs gradually fuse into an ever-expanding central trunk that is characterized by deep furrows and folds. This trunk will often hollow out in old age. In 'Lorton Vale Yew Trees', William Wordsworth described the yew as 'upcoiling' and 'inveterately convolved', which is a poet's way of describing a tree that ties itself in snaking knots. It's not a tree of the streets – in a city you're most likely to find yew in a cemetery or park. It can also be trained into high hedge forms, and some of the most impressive ones I've met have been growing as ornamental hedges in urban botanic gardens.

The yew's evergreen foliage is tight-packed, dense and dark. Short, soft needle-like leaves are arranged in two rows on either side of each twig. Its thick, year-round pelt makes the yew a well-protected nesting place, as well as a good medium for topiary. It bears each of its seeds inside a fleshy, berry-like cup. Although the seed is poisonous, the bright-red flesh that surrounds it is not, and it's a favourite food of blackbirds. The tree's fibrous bark is richly orange-red, sometimes purplish and, if you cut into it, it will weep a sap that looks a lot like blood. In *Meetings with Remarkable Trees*, historian Thomas Pakenham describes its tough, durable pink wood as being as 'springy as steel' and, as such, it was traditionally used to make weapons and tools. In 1911, a spearhead made from yew was found at Clacton-on-Sea in Essex. One of the world's oldest surviving wooden artefacts, this spear is estimated to be about 450,000 years old and is evidence of just how long we have relied on trees and their wood.

::::

Today we need yew to help us fight ill health rather than battles. In the late 1960s, the bark of the Pacific yew was found to contain an anti-tumour alkaloid called taxol, which, despite its toxicity, can be used to treat certain kinds of cancer. Other yew species, including the common yew, have since been found to contain the alkaloid too, in their leaves as well as their bark. Cancer Research UK explains that two chemotherapy drugs were originally developed from yew trees: docetaxel and paclitaxel. Both drugs can now be made synthetically, but yew needles are still used in the manufacturing process. If you happen to be lucky enough to have a yew tree or hedge in your garden that you like to keep in good trim, there are businesses that will collect and pay for your clippings, which they will then sell on to pharmaceutical companies.

Using yew in this way is part of a broader trend. Industrialized nations all but abandoned the use of medicinal plants throughout the twentieth century, but there's been a gradual return to the study of phytochemistry. This makes sense, as plants and trees contain a large number of bioactive compounds – such as polyphenols, flavonoids, phytoestrogens, terpenoids, phytosterols, fatty acids and vitamins – all of which are known to benefit human health. As many as 50 per cent of prescription drugs are based on molecules that occur naturally in plants, including willow for aspirin and cinchona trees for quinine. Pharmaceutical companies looking to create new drugs are finding that an ethno-medical approach, based on traditional healthcare knowledge, is faster and more successful than gathering plants in a more random, less-informed way.

Yews don't produce taxol for our benefit – the chemical is part of a defence mechanism used by the tree to fend off predators. Taxol is powerfully anti-fungal and protects the yew from pathogens that, if left alone, would colonize its tissue. In his essay 'The Intelligent Plant', author and journalist Michael Pollan explains that plants make use of a 'complex molecular vocabulary to signal distress, deter or poison enemies'. Rooted to one spot and unable to run away when under attack, they need an 'extensive and nuanced understanding' of their surroundings and a 'highly developed sensory apparatus' in order to survive and thrive.

The idea of plant intelligence is controversial. Trees are not like mammals, and they don't operate or communicate in the ways we do. However, they do react to their environment and prevailing conditions, and alter their make-up and behaviour accordingly. Pollan explains that much of the current research into how plants behave, which is inspired by the science of networks, distributed computing and swarm theories, has shown 'some of the ways in which remarkably brainy behaviour can emerge in the absence of actual brains'.

A Radiolab documentary called *Smarty Plants* delves into this, reporting on a series of experiments carried out by plant biologist Monica Gagliano. One of them re-created a test similar to that of Ivan Pavlov's famous psychology experiments with dogs. In that case, Pavlov showed that if dogs learned to associate the ringing of a bell with the appearance of food, eventually they would salivate just on hearing the bell, even if there was no meat. Gagliano wondered if she could replicate the experiment with a plant. She swapped the dogs for pea plants, the bell for small electric fans, and the meat for light, which is what plants eat. She knew the peas would lean towards light when it was available, and that the lean was the equivalent of the dogs producing saliva. Placing the pea plants in a darkened room, she set up an experiment where electric fans would go on, lights would go on and the peas would in turn lean towards the light source. *Fans, lights, lean. Fans, lights, lean.* Eventually, after three days of training the plants like this, she decided to see what would happen if she just put the fans on, but didn't provide the food. The pea plants still leaned, anticipating that if the fans were on, the lights soon would be too. They had learned to associate the fan with food, just like the dogs had with the bell. Gagliano admits she doesn't yet know how the plants do this, and that there are more questions here than answers, but she doesn't think the fact they don't have brains is a big deal.

In a TED talk that he gave a few years before writing his 'Intelligent Plant' essay, Michael Pollan encourages us to look at the world from other species' perspectives. He challenges our self-importance too, arguing that – rather than being something that separates us from, and sets us above, other living things – consciousness is simply 'another set of tools for getting along in the world'. And while we have it, along with language and tool-making, plants have biochemistry, something just as complex and sophisticated, and which 'they have perfected ... to a degree far beyond what we can imagine'.

⁙

I decide to spend some time with a yew I know in a park near where I live, and I find that Pollan's arguments and Gagliano's experiments have altered how I feel about it. I still admire its grand old age and poetic good looks, and the fact that it is the source of an important cancer-fighting drug, but beyond all the things it does that somehow pleases us – be that aesthetically or medically – I also now appreciate just how clever it is in its own right. I find myself trying to understand it on its own terms, rather than mine; attempting to relate to it rather than merely look at it. It depends on your definition of intelligence as to whether or not a plant can have it, but if you will agree to something that is not brain-bound but is instead the ability to respond to the challenges presented by one's circumstances, then it's definitely something that plants, including the mighty taxol-producing yew tree, possess. Accepting this changes our relationship with the flora around us, whether that's in the city or in the country. It requires us to see ourselves and plants on much more equal terms.

ANOTHER MEDICALLY SIGNIFICANT TREE WORTH KNOWING

A willow that you're likely to see in the city is the weeping one (*Salix babylonica*). It's a large, magnificent tree, with rope-like branches and long, narrow leaves that are pale underneath. It has a graceful, drooping silhouette and is found planted along waterways and beside lakes and ponds. Its long roots help hold banks in place. Willows are celebrated for their slender, flexible stems, which can be woven into baskets and boats. They're also what cricket bats are made from, and the sound of leather on willow is the sound of summer for some people. The bark of willow trees contains acetylsalicylic acid, an anti-inflammatory traditionally used to ease stiff and painful joints. It's the compound that aspirin is based on.

Ending

While I was writing this book, Sheffield's street trees suffered. Even the sentimental among us can accept that surgery is sometimes necessary with age, and that a street tree can become a hazard and need to be removed, but what was happening in Sheffield wasn't routine maintenance, it was a cull. Decisions about a tree's fate were being made in cloak-and-dagger ways, and the chainsaws were often coming out at night on dates unannounced in advance.

Tree groups formed across Sheffield, made up of people determined to stop the felling. They wanted to secure a strategy for street-tree management in their city which recognized that replacing a 100-year-old tree with a sapling was not a like-for-like swap. Interviewed by the *Daily Mail* about a grand old elm on Chelsea Road in Nether Edge, Matt Larsen-Daw of the Woodland Trust argued that 'In environmental terms, taking down this elm and replacing it with a sapling is like taking down the Royal Albert Hall and putting up a tent.' The newspaper also interviewed the Green Party councillor Alison Teal, who said of her colleagues on the council, 'When you talk to them about the Chelsea Road elm they just say: "An elm belongs in a forest, not in a street."' As thousands of mature but misunderstood street trees were cut down across Sheffield, those doomed to fall next were decorated with pom-poms, ribbons and love letters. Many ordinary people, including Alison Teal, protested peacefully and faced arrest, court cases, injunctions and fines as a result.

For the most part I was hundreds of miles away, increasingly with my head in my hands. As I learned more about the wonders of the urban ecosystem, and the value that urban trees have, I understood less and less why a city would actively choose to lose so much of its mega-flora. The deforesting of Sheffield – a British city long loved for being one of our leafiest – revealed that urban trees are far from being universally cherished, and that caring for the urban forest isn't always considered worth the expense. It demonstrated that organizations driven by financial profit are often not good custodians of the environment. It also showed that stripping a city of some its oldest and most gnarled members will strip out some of that city's soul and run a hot spear right through residents' hearts. Feelings for urban trees run deep – much deeper than Sheffield City Council or its private contractor, Amey, could possibly have imagined. Outrage at their felling programme, which spread nationwide, eventually attracting the attention of the Secretary of State for the Environment, underlined how much a city's trees are part of its identity, and that our urban forests are utterly worth our time.

::::

In *The Secret Life of Trees*, Colin Tudge says, 'each of us might aspire to be a connoisseur of nature, and connoisseurship implies a combination of knowledge on the one hand and love on the other, each enhancing the other'. I see this as a call to action to all of us: to understand and respect trees, and everything they do for us. Sheffield's tree defenders are true connoisseurs.

As I've aspired for a connoisseurship of my own (there will always be more to learn), I've discovered that you have to be brave to take on a subject when you're not an expert, but that striving to know more and telling people about it is an activism of sorts. And while taxonomy is inherently anthropocentric, and says as much about us and our need to control things as it does about animals and plants, it can also be a friendly act and the beginning of a long relationship. As Nan Shepherd says in *The Living Mountain*, 'Knowing another is endless ... The thing to be known grows with the knowing.'

Getting to know some of the species I see around town is bringing me and the trees closer, just like I hoped it would.

Bibliography

It was a pleasure and an education researching *Sylvan Cities*. The resources listed below were invaluable, and this book wouldn't have been possible without them. All are recommended as further reading, listening and viewing.

FIELD GUIDES

Aas, Gregor and Andreas Riedmiller, *Trees of Britain and Europe*, HarperCollins, 1994

'Discover British Trees', Woodland Trust; woodlandtrust.org.uk/visiting-woods/trees-woods-and-wildlife/british-trees

Fitter, Alastair and David More, *Trees*, HarperCollins, 2012

'Hyde Park, Walks for tree lovers', The Royal Parks Foundation

Johnson, Owen and David More, *Collins Tree Guide*, HarperCollins, 2006

Phillips, Roger, *Trees in Britain, Europe and North America,* Pan Books, 1981

GENERAL GUIDES

Briggs, Gertrude, *A Brief History of Trees*, Max Press, 2016

Cohu, Will, *Out of the Woods*, Short Books, 2007

Conway, Peter, *Tree Medicine, A comprehensive guide to the healing power of over 170 trees*, Piatkus, 2001

Mabey, Richard, *Flora Britannica*, Chatto & Windus, 1996

—— *The Unofficial Countryside*, Little Toller Books, 2010

—— *The Ash and the Beech, The Drama of Woodland Change*, Vintage, 2013

—— *The Cabaret of Plants*, Profile, 2015

Pakenham, Thomas, *Meetings with Remarkable Trees*, Phoenix Illustrated, 1997

Rackham, Oliver, *Trees & Woodland in the British Landscape*, revised edition, Dent, 1990

Stafford, Fiona, *The Long, Long Life of Trees*, Yale, 2017

Tudge, Colin, *The Secret Life of Trees, How They Live and Why They Matter*, Penguin, 2006

Wohlleben, Peter, *The Hidden Life of Trees, What They Feel, How They Communicate*, Greystone Books, 2016

Wood, Paul, *London's Street Trees, A Field Guide to the Urban Forest*, Safe Haven, 2017

Chapter by chapter

OPENING QUOTE

Thompson, Della (ed.), *The Concise Oxford Dictionary of Current English*, ninth edition, Clarendon Press, 1995

BEGINNING

Ackroyd, Peter, *London, The Biography*, Vintage, 2001

Babbs, Helen, 'Urban wallpaper', *Lost in London*, winter 2013

Britt, Chris and Mark Johnston, 'Trees in Towns II, A new survey of urban trees in England and their condition and management', Department for Communities and Local Government, 2008

Burdett, Ricky and Deyan Sudjic (eds.), 'Living in the Urban Age', *Living in the Endless City, The Urban Age Project*, London School of Economics and Deutsche Bank's Alfred Herrhausen Society, Phaidon, 2011

Coleridge, Samuel Taylor, 'This Lime-Tree Bower My Prison', The Poetry Foundation; poetryfoundation.org/poems/43992/this-lime-tree-bower-my-prison

'Connecting with nature offers a new approach to mental health care', Natural England, 9 February 2016

Doick, Kieron, Jessica Goodenough, Kenton Rogers and Keith Sacre, 'Valuing London's Urban Forest, Results of the London I-Tree Eco Project', Treeconomics, 2015

Dostoevsky, Fyodor, *Winter Notes on Summer Impressions*, Alma Classics, 2016

Evans, David, 'Prehistory', '1970s: Going public and getting places', *A History of Nature Conservation in Britain*, second edition, Routledge, 1997

Heath, Francis George, *Our British Trees and How to Know Them*, fifth edition, Hutchinson & Co., 1907

Johnston, Mark, 'The Rise of Professional Arboriculture', 'Threats to Urban Trees', *Trees in Towns and Cities, A History of British Urban Arboriculture*, Windgather Press, 2015

——— and Lia D. Shimada, 'Urban Forestry in a Multicultural Society', *Journal of Arboriculture*, May 2004

Kuo, Frances E. Ming, 'Parks and Other Green Environments: Essential Components of a Healthy Human Habitat', University of Illinois, 2010

Mabey, Richard, 'Heartwoods', 'The Immediate Effect of Wood', *The Ash and the Beech, The Drama of Woodland Change*, Vintage, 2013

Montgomery, Charles, 'How to be Closer', *Happy City, Transforming Our Lives Through Urban Design*, Penguin, 2013

'Nature and Wellbeing Act, A Green Paper from the Wildlife Trusts and the RSPB', The Wildlife Trusts and the Royal Society for the Protection of Birds, 29 October 2014

Nilsson, K., M. Sangster, C. Gallis, T. Hartig, S. de Vries, K. Seeland and J. Schipperijn (ed), 'Urban Forests and Their Ecosystem Services in Relation to Human Health', *Forests, Trees and Human Health*, Springer, 2010

Ponting, Clive, 'The Rise of the City', *A New Green History of the World, The Environment and the Collapse of Great Civilisations*, Vintage, 2007

'Urban Forests and Climate Change', USDA; fs.usda.gov/ccrc/topics/urban-forests-and-climate-change

Wallop, Harry, 'Britain's public parks: 175 years old, but will they survive?', *The Telegraph*, 3 October 2015

ALDER

Calvino, Italo, *Invisible Cities*, Vintage Classics, 1997

Jamie, Kathleen, 'The Alder', *The Tree House*, Picador, 2014

Wohlleben, Peter, *The Hidden Life of Trees, What They Feel, How They Communicate*, Greystone Books, 2016

ITALIAN ALDER

Cohu, Will, 'Glimpsed from a Car', *Out of the Woods*, Short Books, 2007

Johnson, Owen and David More, 'Italian alder', *Collins Tree Guide*, HarperCollins, 2006

ASH

Albertini, Doick, Hutchings, Rumble and Rogers, 'Valuing urban trees in Glasgow, Assessing the ecosystem services of Glasgow's urban forest: a technical report', Glasgow City Council and Forestry Commission, June 2015

'Ash Dieback 2012', Tree timeline, *LEAF!*, Common Ground, spring 2017

'Askr and Embla', *Encyclopaedia Britannica*; britannica.com/topic/Askr-and-Embla

'A Tree in Argyle Street', Hidden Glasgow Forums; hiddenglasgow.com/forums

Cowan, James, *From Glasgow's Treasure Chest*, Craig & Wilson, 1951

Crump, Vincent, 'Ashes to ashes: the inevitable impact of ash dieback', *Broadleaf No. 91*, The Woodland Trust, winter 2018

Goode, David, 'Vestiges of the Natural World', *Wild in London*, Michael Joseph, 1986

Juniper, Tony, *What Nature Does for Britain*, Profile, 2015

Mabey, Richard, 'The Vegetable Plot', *The Cabaret of Plants*, Profile, 2015

McKenna, Kevin, 'Kevin McKenna on the rebirth of Finnieston in Glasgow', *The Herald*, 21 November 2015

Paul4Jags, 'Assignments, Trees in cities: share your photos and stories, A solitary ash tree, Glasgow', *The Guardian Witness*, 2015

Rival, Laura (ed.), 'Preface', *The Social Life of Trees, Anthropological Perspectives on Tree Symbolism*, Berg, 2001

Shepherd, Nan, *The Living Mountain*, Canongate, 2008

Stafford, Fiona, 'Venus of the Woods', *The Paris Review*, 4 October 2016

Trigg, Dylan, 'On Alex Katz's *Night Branch*', *Tate Etc.*, issue 38, autumn 2016

RAYWOOD ASH

Wood, Paul, 'Raywood Ash', *London's Street Trees, A Field Guide to the Urban Forest*, Safe Haven, 2017

BEECH

Frazer, James George, 'The Worship of Trees', *The Golden Bough, A Study in Magic and Religion*, Oxford World Classics, 2008

Kennedy, Kelsey, 'The Mysterious Tree Carvings of America's Basque Sheepherders', *Atlas Obscura*, 3 October 2017

Mabey, Richard, 'The Lowest Trees have Tops', 'Feeling Through the Eyes', *The Ash and the Beech, The Drama of Woodland Change*, Vintage, 2013

Maitland, Sara, *Gossip from the Forest, The Tangled Roots of Our Forests and Fairytales*, Granta, 2012

Orwell, George, *Keep the Aspidistra Flying*, Penguin Modern Classics, 2014

Rackham, Oliver, *Trees & Woodland in the British Landscape*, revised edition, Dent, 1990

'WW2 tree carvings and bark graffiti unveil private lives from the past', *The Telegraph*, 29 May 2012

BIRCH

Abhijith, K.V. et al., 'Air pollution abatement performances of green infrastructure in open road and built-up street canyon environments. A review', *Atmospheric Environment*, 162, 2017

'Alvar Aalto, Paimio Chair, 1931–32', The Museum of Modern Art, New York; moma.org/collection/works/92879

Frost, Robert, 'Birches', The Poetry Foundation; poetryfoundation.org/poems/44260/birches

'Plywood: Material of the Modern World', Victoria and Albert Museum, 15 July 2017–12 November 2017

'The Big Air Pollution Experiment', *Trust Me, I'm a Doctor*, BBC, 2013

BUTTERFLY BUSH

Babbs, Helen, 'Gardens: buddleia', *The Guardian*, 6 July 2012

Nabokov, Vladimir, 'Butterflies', *The New Yorker*, 12 June 1948

'Position statement on Buddleia and its planting in the UK', Butterfly Conservation, 3 November 2012

Rotherham, Ian D., 'Times they are a changin' – Recombinant Ecology as an emerging paradigm', Sheffield Hallam University, 2015

LEYLAND CYPRESS

Britt, C. and M. Johnston, Executive Summary, 'Trees in Towns II, A new survey of urban trees in England and their condition and management', Department for Communities and Local Government, 2008

'Leylandii: Why are they still so popular?', BBC News website, 27 September 2011

Stafford, Fiona, 'Cypress', *The Long, Long Life of Trees*, Yale, 2017

Turrell, Nick, 'Gardens: leylandii', *The Guardian*, 7 December 2012

CHERRY

Carson, Rachel, *The Sense of Wonder*, HarperCollins, 1997

Cohu, Will, 'Cherry Blossom Comrades', *Out of the Woods*, Short Books, 2007

Johnston, Mark, 'Planting "Post-Conflict" Landscapes: Urban Trees in Peacebuilding and Reconstruction', Conference paper, April 2014

O'Connor, Joanne, 'Trees of life', *The Observer Magazine*, 6 May 2018

'Prunus Pissardii', Royal Horticultural Society; rhs.org.uk/Plants/99810/i-Prunus-cerasifera-i-Pissardii/Details

Rudhyar, Dane, *Directives for New Life*, 1971, as quoted in 'Should Trees Have Standing? Towards Legal Rights for Natural Objects', Christopher D. Stone, *Southern California Law Review*, 45, 1972

Sackville-West, Vita, *Let Us Now Praise Famous Gardens*, Penguin, 2009

Stafford, Fiona, 'Cherry', *The Long, Long Life of Trees*, Yale, 2017

Wilson, E. O., *Biophilia, The human bond with other species*, Harvard University Press, 1984

Wood, Paul, 'Flowering Cherries', *London's Street Trees, A Field Guide to the Urban Forest*, Safe Haven, 2017

ELDER

Berger, John, *Why Look at Animals?*, Penguin, 2009

Conway, Peter, 'Sambucus nigra', *Tree Medicine, A comprehensive guide to the healing power of over 170 trees*, Piatkus, 2001

De Botton, Alain, 'Consolation for Frustration', *The Consolations of Philosophy*, Penguin, 2001

Flood, Alison, 'Oxford Junior Dictionary's replacement of "natural" words with 21st-century terms sparks outcry', *The Guardian*, 13 January 2015

Fowles, John, *The Tree*, Vintage, 2000

Handmade Apothecary: handmadeapothecary.co.uk

Haskell, David George, *The Songs of Trees, Stories from Nature's Great Connectors*, Viking, 2017

Linnaeus, Carl, *Philosophia Botanica*, 1751, as quoted in 'Making Nature, How we see animals' at the Wellcome Collection, 1 December 2016–21 May 2017

McCarthy, Michael, 'We've killed botany, let's save the flowers', *The Guardian*, 10 May 2016

Murray, Dick, 'Passengers choke on the Tube', *Evening Standard*, 23 August 2002

Nex, Sally, 'Death knell sounds for botany degrees', *The Garden*, January 2012

Nilsson, K., M. Sangster, C. Gallis, T. Hartig, S. de Vries, K. Seeland and J. Schipperijn (eds), 'Forest Products with Health-Promoting and Medicinal Properties', *Forests, Trees and Human Health*, Springer, 2010

Wilson, E. O., *Biophilia, The human bond with other species*, Harvard University Press, 1984

ELM

'Brighton's Elm Tree Collection', Visit Brighton and University of Brighton

Greenland, Rob, 'Brighton's Elm Trees'; brightonelmtrees.com

Martin, Arthur, 'Mystery of the tree covered in shoes … and £265,000 of lottery funding can't solve it', *Daily Mail*, 8 January 2009

Richens, R. H., *Elm*, Cambridge University Press, 1983

Sebald, W. G., *The Rings of Saturn*, Vintage, 2002

'Shoe tree mystery defeats £265,000 investigation', *The Telegraph*, 8 January 2009

'Shoe trees', Roadside America; roadsideamerica.com/story/29064

Stafford, Fiona, 'Elm', *The Long, Long Life of Trees*, Yale, 2017

FIG

Bramwell, David, 'A forest of figs', *Waterfront blog*, Canal and River Trust, 26 November 2015

Fothergill, Alastair, 'Rainforests. Everyone's Favourite Fruit', *Planet Earth*, BBC Books, 2006

Frazer, James George, 'The Worship of Trees', *The Golden Bough, A Study in Magic and Religion*, Oxford World Classics, 2008

Gilbert, Oliver, *The Ecology of Urban Habitats*, Springer, 1989

'Hadfield's Weir', Five Weirs Walk, riverside interpretation boards, Sheffield City Council, Ramblers and Peak & Northern Footpaths Society

Mabey, Richard, *Flora Britannica*, Chatto & Windus, 1996

'Oliver Gilbert, Lichen hunter and urban ecologist in the wildlife jungle of Sheffield', *The Independent*, 17 May 2005

'The Amwell Fig', *Great Trees of London*, Time Out Guides, 2010

'The River Don: Hadfield Weir Fish Pass', riverside interpretation board, Don Catchment Rivers Trust

Wakefield, Robin, as reported by Charlotte Higgins, 'The oddest classical etymologies ever?', *The Guardian*, 23 March 2009

MULBERRY

Sebald, W. G., *The Rings of Saturn*, Vintage, 2002

HAZEL

Hunt, Margaret, 'The Hazel Branch (Die Haselrute)', *Household Tales by the Brothers Grimm*; gutenberg.org/ebooks/5314

Leeds Coppice Workers: leedscoppiceworkers.co.uk

Maitland, Sara, *Gossip from the Forest, The Tangled Roots of Our Forests and Fairytales*, Granta, 2012

Mancuso, Stefano, as quoted by Michael Pollan, 'The Intelligent Plant, Scientists debate a new way of understanding flora', *The New Yorker*, 23 & 30 December 2013

Rackham, Oliver, *Trees & Woodland in the British Landscape*, revised edition, Dent, 1990

Rival, Laura (ed.), 'Preface', *The Social Life of Trees, Anthropological Perspectives on Tree Symbolism*, Berg, 2001

TURKISH HAZEL

Johnson, Owen and David More, 'Turkish hazel', *Collins Tree Guide*, HarperCollins, 2006

Wood, Paul, 'Turkish Hazel', *London's Street Trees, A Field Guide to the Urban Forest*, Safe Haven, 2017

HORSE CHESTNUT

'Anne Frank Tree': annefrank.org

Coles, Jeremy, 'Why we love conkers and horse chestnut trees', BBC Earth, 9 October 2015

Conway, Peter, *Tree Medicine, A comprehensive guide to the healing power of over 170 trees*, Piatkus, 2001

Frank, Anne, *The Diary of a Young Girl*, Puffin, 2007

Sartre, Jean-Paul, *Nausea*, Penguin, 2000

'The Wood Street Horse Chestnut', 'The chestnut: horse versus sweet', *Great Trees of London*, Time Out Guides, 2010

SWEET CHESTNUT

Johnson, Owen and David More, 'Sweet chestnut', *Collins Tree Guide*, HarperCollins, 2006

'The chestnut: horse versus sweet', *Great Trees of London*, Time Out Guides, 2010

LIME

Adnan, Etel, 'from The Manifestations of the Voyage', The Poetry Foundation; poetryfoundation.org/poems/53852/from-the-manifestations-of-the-voyage

—— 'Linden Trees', editmanar.com/auteurs/Linden%20trees.htm

Berger, John, 'The White Bird', *Why Look at Animals?*, Penguin, 2009

Conway, Peter, *Tree Medicine, A comprehensive guide to the healing power of over 170 trees*, Piatkus, 2001

Dove, Rita, 'Ludwig Van Beethoven's Return to Vienna', Lyrik-line; lyrikline.org/en/poems/ludwig-van-beethovens-return-vienna-5919

Pakenham, Thomas, 'The Best and Worst of Limes', *Meetings with Remarkable Trees*, Phoenix Illustrated, 1997

Plotkin, Fred, 'Following Beethoven's Footsteps in Vienna', Operavore, WQXR, 14 November 2011

Proust, Marcel, *Remembrance of Things Past*, translated by C. K. Scott Moncrieff, Wordsworth Editions, 2006

Rackham, Oliver, *Trees & Woodland in the British Landscape*, revised edition, Dent, 1990

Wiener, Eric, 'Genius is Unintentional. Vienna: Pitch Perfect', *The Geography of Genius, A Search for the World's Most Creative Places from Ancient Athens to Silicon Valley*, Simon & Schuster, 2016

Williams, Florence, 'The Cordial Air', *The Nature Fix, Why Nature Makes Us Happier, Healthier and More Creative*, W. W. Norton & Company, 2017

Wood, Paul, 'An Introduction to the Urban Forest', guided walk and talk, London Tree Week 2017

MAIDENHAIR

Ballard, J. G., *The Drowned World*, Fourth Estate, 2014

Campbell, Lindsay K., Heather L. McMillen and Erika S. Svendsen, 'Co-creators of Memory, Metaphors for Resilience, and Mechanisms for Recovery: Flora in Living Memorials to 9/11', *Journal of Ethnobiology*, 2017

Dorfman, Ariel, 'The Whispering Leaves of the Hiroshima Ginkgo Trees', *New York Times*, 4 August 2017

Gough, Paul, 'From Heroes' Groves to Parks of Peace: Landscapes of remembrance, protest and peace', *Landscape Research*, 2000

Grahame, Kenneth, *The Wind in the Willows*, Puffin, 2008

Mabey, Richard, *The Ash and the Beech, The Drama of Woodland Change*, Vintage, 2013

Pakenham, Thomas, 'Going Downhill for 60 Million Years', *Meetings with Remarkable Trees*, Phoenix Illustrated, 1997

Wood, Paul, 'Ginkgo', *London's Street Trees, A Field Guide to the Urban Forest*, Safe Haven, 2017

CAUCASIAN WINGNUT

Johnson, Owen and David More, 'Caucasian wingnut', *Collins Tree Guide*, HarperCollins, 2006

MAPLE

Briggs, Gertrude, *A Brief History of Trees*, Max Press, 2016

Clare, John, 'The Maple Tree', Poem Hunter; poemhunter.com/best-poems/john-clare/the-maple-tree/

Cohu, Will, *Out of the Woods*, Short Books, 2007

'Delays Explained: leaves', Network Rail; networkrail.co.uk/running-the-railway/looking-after-the-railway/delays-explained/leaves

Doick, Kieron, Jessica Goodenough, Kenton Rogers and Keith Sacre, 'Valuing London's Urban Forest, Results of the London I-Tree Eco Project', Treeconomics, 2015

—— P. Handley, F. Ashwood, M. Vaz Monteiro, K. Frediani and K. Rogers, 'Valuing Edinburgh's Urban Trees. An update to the 2011 i-Tree Eco survey – a report of Edinburgh City Council and Forestry Commission Scotland', Forest Research, 2017

East, Ben, 'Holloway by Robert Macfarlane, Stanley Donwood and Dan Richards – review', *The Observer*, 1 June 2013

Laville, Sandra, 'Call to halt tree felling as new rail cull exposed', *The Guardian*, 10 May 2018

'Leonardo da Vinci's Helicopter', 'Leonardo da Vinci's Tank', 'Leonardo da Vinci's Glider', leonardodavincisinventions.com

Parkland Walk: parkland-walk.org.uk

Raban, Jonathan, 'Second Nature, The de-landscaping of the American West', *The New Nature Writing, Granta* 102, summer 2008

Ratcliffe, Susan, *Oxford Essential Quotations*, Oxford University Press, 2016; oxfordreference.com

Stafford, Fiona, 'Sycamore', *The Long, Long Life of Trees*, Yale, 2017

Water of Leith: wateroﬂeith.org.uk

OAK

Babbs, Helen, 'Gardens: soil', *The Guardian*, 4 April 2014

Conway, Peter, 'The Forest Pharmacy – How Tree Medicine Works', 'Quercus robur', *Tree Medicine, A comprehensive guide to the healing power of over 170 trees*, Piatkus, 2001

Doick, Kieron, Jessica Goodenough, Kenton Rogers and Keith Sacre, 'Valuing London's Urban Forest, Results of the London I-Tree Eco Project', Treeconomics, 2015

Fiennes, Peter, 'Tree reasons why ancient oaks survived the felling of ancient forests in Britain', *The Ecologist*, 11 September 2017

'From Tree to Shining Tree', Radiolab, 30 July 2016; radiolab.org/story/from-tree-to-shining-tree

Giordano, Chiara, 'The land of leather: Bermondsey's history of leather making', *Southwark News*, 2 February 2017

Greer, Germaine, 'What is a Tree? Stump Cross, Essex', *Arboreal, A Collection of New Woodland Writing*, Little Toller Books, 2016

Hardy, Thomas, *The Woodlanders*, Oxford Classics, 2009

Mayhew, Henry, 'Letter LXXVIII. Friday, November 15, 1850', *The Morning Chronicle Survey of Labour and the Poor. The Metropolitan Districts*, vol. 6, Routledge Library Editions: The History of Social Welfare

Rackham, Oliver, *Trees & Woodland in the British Landscape*, revised edition, Dent, 1990

Simard, Suzanne, 'How trees talk to each other', TED, June 2016; ted.com/talks/suzanne_simard_how_trees_talk_to_each_other

Wohlleben, Peter, *The Hidden Life of Trees, What They Feel, How They Communicate*, Greystone Books, 2016

PINE

Barkham, Patrick, 'If you go down to the woods today ...', *The Guardian*, 21 January 2017

Briggs, Gertrude, *A Brief History of Trees*, Max Press, 2016

Conway, Peter, *Tree Medicine, A comprehensive guide to the healing power of over 170 trees*, Piatkus, 2001

Cooper, Adrian and Robert Macfarlane, 'Uprooted', *The Clearing*, Little Toller Books, 16 July 2016

Fairlie, Simon, 'A Short History of Enclosure in Britain', *The Land*, summer 2009

'Forestry Commission 1919', Tree timeline, *LEAF!*, Common Ground, spring 2017

'Forestry Statistics 2017, Chapter 1: Woodland Areas and Planting', Forestry Commission, 2017

Granville, Augustus, 'Bournemouth', *The Spas of England and Principal Sea-Bathing Places*, Henry Colburn Publisher, 1841

'History of Alum Chine', beachside noticeboard

Juniper, Tony, *What Nature Does for Britain*, Profile, 2015

Mabey, Richard, 'Vivat Regina', *The Ash and the Beech, The Drama of Woodland Change*, Vintage, 2013

Martinez-Conde, Susana and Stephen L. Macknik, 'Illusory Faces Peer Out of Unlikely Places', *Scientific American*, 1 September 2012

'Pines of Bournemouth', South Coast Central; south-coast-central.co.uk/pines

Rackham, Oliver, *Trees & Woodland in the British Landscape*, revised edition, Dent, 1990

Robson, David, 'Neuroscience: why do we see faces in everyday objects?', BBC Future, 30 July 2014

Rosen, Rebecca, 'Pareidolia: A Bizarre Bug of the Human Mind Emerges in Computers', *The Atlantic*, 7 August 2012

Simmons, I. G., 'A Fit Country for Heroes, 1914–50', 'A Post-Industrial World, 1950 to the Present', *An Environmental History of Great Britain, From 10,000 years ago to the Present*, Edinburgh University Press, 2001

Wohlleben, Peter, *The Hidden Life of Trees, What They Feel, How They Communicate*, Greystone Books, 2016

PLANE

Ackroyd, Peter, 'The natural history of London', *London, The Biography*, Vintage, 2001

Barkham, Patrick, 'Story of cities #34: the struggle for the soul of Milton Keynes', *The Guardian*, 3 May 2016

Conway, Peter, *Tree Medicine, A comprehensive guide to the healing power of over 170 trees*, Piatkus, 2001

Doick, Kieron, Jessica Goodenough, Kenton Rogers and Keith Sacre, 'Valuing London's Urban Forest, Results of the London I-Tree Eco Project', Treeconomics, 2015

Fowles, John, *The Tree*, Vintage, 2000

Greer, Germaine, 'What is a Tree? Stump Cross, Essex', *Arboreal, A Collection of New Woodland Writing*, Little Toller Books, 2016

Mabey, Richard, 'Feeling Through the Eyes', *The Ash and the Beech, The Drama of Woodland Change*, Vintage, 2013

SWEET GUM

Wood, Paul, 'American Sweetgum', *London's Street Trees, A Field Guide to the Urban Forest*, Safe Haven, 2017

POPLAR

Johnston, Mark, 'Threats to Urban Trees', *Trees in Towns and Cities, A History of British Urban Arboriculture*, Windgather Press, 2015

Manchester Museum Herbarium: museum.manchester.ac.uk/collection/plants/

'Manchester Poplar', Manchester Guided Tours; manchesterguidedtours.com

'Millennium Seed Bank', 'Seed Collection', Kew; kew.org

'Native Black Poplar, *Populus nigra subsp. betulifolia*', Biodiversity Action Plan for Greater Manchester

Rackham, Oliver, *Trees & Woodland in the British Landscape*, revised edition, Dent, 1990

Stafford, Fiona, 'Poplar', *The Long, Long Life of Trees*, Yale, 2017

TREE OF HEAVEN

Davies, Rob, 'The toxic Tree of Heaven threatens England's green and pleasant land', *The Guardian*, 17 September 2016

Gay, Oona and Sue McCarthy, 'Ada Salter: Beautifying Bermondsey', guided walk and talk, Bermondsey Street Festival 2017

Smith, Betty, *A Tree Grows in Brooklyn*, Arrow, 2000

Wood, Paul, 'An Introduction to the Urban Forest', guided walk and talk, London Tree Week 2017

—— 'Tree of Heaven', *London's Street Trees, A Field Guide to the Urban Forest*, Safe Haven, 2017

INDIAN BEAN TREE

'Catalpa bignonioides', Royal Horticultural Society; rhs.org.uk/ Plants/3201/Catalpa-bignonioides/Details

WHITEBEAM

'Bristol Whitebeam', University of Bristol; bristol.ac.uk/centenary/look/ cabinet/bristol-whitebeam.html

Butler, Robert, 'In the mud with Richard Long', *1843, The Economist*, autumn 2008

Dunmore, Helen, 'City, Trees, Water. Avon Gorge, Bristol', *Arboreal, A Collection of New Woodland Writing*, Little Toller Books, 2016

Hawkins, Alexander, 'Wayfaring land artist Richard Long pays homage to his Bristol roots', *It's Nice That*, 3 August 2015

'Richard Long: Time and Space', Arnolfini gallery, 31 July 2015–15 November 2015

'Sorbus bristoliensis (Bristol Whitebeam)', IUCN Red List of Threatened Species; iucnredlist.org/details/34741/0

'Sorbus bristoliensis (Bristol Whitebeam)', ukwildflowers.com

Watkins, Jack, 'Whitebeams spread their leaves in Bristol's Avon Gorge',
The Telegraph, 14 May 2009

Wood, Paul, 'An Introduction to the Urban Forest', guided walk and talk,
London Tree Week 2017

YEW

'Clacton Spearhead 450,000 BCE', *LEAF!*, Common Ground, spring 2017

Nilsson, K., M. Sangster, C. Gallis, T. Hartig, S. de Vries, K. Seeland and
J. Schipperijn (eds), 'Forest Products with Health-Promoting and
Medicinal Properties', *Forests, Trees and Human Health*, Springer, 2010

Pakenham, Thomas, 'Gloom or Bloom at Much Marcle', *Meetings with
Remarkable Trees*, Phoenix Illustrated, 1997

Pollan, Michael, 'A plant's-eye view', TED, 2007; ted.com/talks/michael_
pollan_gives_a_plant_s_eye_view

—— 'The Intelligent Plant, Scientists debate a new way of understanding
flora', *The New Yorker*, 23 & 30 December 2013

'Smarty Plants', Radiolab, 14 February 2018; radiolab.org/story/smarty-
plants

Stafford, Fiona, 'Yew', *The Long, Long Life of Trees*, Yale, 2017

Talbot, Nicholas J., 'Plant Immunity: A Little Help from Fungal Friends',
Current Biology, vol. 25, issue 22, 16 November 2015

Wordsworth, William, 'Lorton Vale Yew Trees', bartleby.com/270/1/285.
html

'Yew clippings', Cancer Research UK; cancerresearchuk.org/about-
cancer/cancer-in-general/treatment/chemotherapy/yew-clippings

WILLOW

Conway, Peter, 'Aspirin', 'Salix alba', *Tree Medicine, A comprehensive guide to
the healing power of over 170 trees*, Piatkus, 2001

Nilsson, K., M. Sangster, C. Gallis, T. Hartig, S. de Vries, K. Seeland and
J. Schipperijn (eds), 'Urban Forests and Their Ecosystem Services in
Relation to Human Health', *Forests, Trees and Human Health*, Springer,
2010

ENDING

Halliday, Josh, 'Green party councillor arrested at Sheffield tree protest',
    The Guardian, 6 February 2017

Hardman, Robert, 'The Chainsaw Massacre', *Daily Mail*, 8 July 2017

Owen, Jonathan, 'Campaign to save Sheffield's trees reaches High Court',
    The Independent, 22 March 2016

Save Sheffield's Trees: savesheffieldtrees.org.uk

Shepherd, Nan, *The Living Mountain*, Canongate, 2008

Tudge, Colin, 'Preface', *The Secret Life of Trees, How They Live and Why They
    Matter*, Penguin, 2006

Acknowledgements

This book has been shaped and informed by some brilliant people. I would like to say a special thank you to Tanya Perdikou, James Roxburgh and Lauren Gardner for their constructive criticism and good advice. For their time and generosity, I'd also like to thank Vicky Chown and Kim Walker, founders of the Handmade Apothecary; Leslie Day, my fellow boater and tree-lover in New York City; Jerry Dicker, my Field Studies Council tree teacher in Scotland; Daniel Greenwood, warden of Sydenham Hill Wood; Rachel Webster, curator of botany at Manchester Museum; and Dave from Leeds Coppice Workers. Finally, a big thank you to Tom Clarke, Clare Coyne, Rosie Coyne, Ria Hopkinson, Jacqueline Peacock and most especially Simon Drake. You all know why.